FIRST STEPS IN TEACHING CREATIVE DANCE TO CHILDREN

children

SECOND EDITION

First Steps in Teaching Creative Dance

Mary Joyce

Photographs by Patty Haley

 MAYFIELD PUBLISHING COMPANY

to Children

Library of Congress Catalog Card Number: 79-91834
International Standard Book Number: 0-87484-510-6

Manufactured in the United States of America
Mayfield Publishing Company
285 Hamilton Avenue, Palo Alto, California 94301

This book was set in Bembo, with display type in Avant Garde
and Tango, by Viking Typographics. It was printed and bound
by Publishers Press. Sponsoring editor was C. Lansing Hays,
Maggie Cutler supervised editing, and manuscript editor was
Zipporah Collins. Book and cover design by Nancy Sears and
layout by Mary Wiley; Michelle Hogan supervised production.

Contents

v

A child steps eagerly into the world of dance

In a class, he is free to move

He experiments with his own energy, with time, with space

He discovers the language of movement

He begins to speak through his body

1

The Theory

WHAT IS CREATIVE DANCE?

Dance is so many things! It can be a leap for joy, a series of steps set to music, a religious ritual, or a work of art. It can be anything from the prance of mating pigeons to Pavlova's "dying swan."

People dance socially. They dance to entertain. They also dance to communicate their deepest feelings. This is the goal of creative dance: *to communicate through movement.*

Dancers learn skills and become expert at executing difficult patterns or steps; but, unless they are eloquent in their expression through movement, their art is incomplete. The language of dance is movement. The instrument is the human body. In creative dance there is no "right" or "wrong." There are no routines to learn. What is important in creative dance is that the dancer draw upon inner resources to make a direct and clear statement. An increase in skill increases ability to communicate, but in creative dance the statement comes before the technique. The individual is the first source; in teaching, you seek to reach the part of the individual that is a composer rather than a player, an originator rather than an interpreter, a creator rather than a performer.

Dance does not blossom full blown in an instant. Most people are not that closely in touch with their souls. They must find a starting place. They need first to become familiar with the art of dance and its craft. They need to develop a language of movement. This book, then, is based on the craft of self-expression. Working with the craft opens the pathway for expression of the inner being.

For the professional dance performer, the road to dance begins with training of the instrument, the body. In creative dance, the road begins with exploration of the *elements of dance*. What are these elements? You are already familiar with them. Children are well aware of them, too. But you may not have thought of them as elements of dance.

THE ELEMENTS OF DANCE

Whenever a person moves, the *body* uses *space, force,* and *time.* These are the four basic elements of dance. Creative dance sessions explore all the possibilities inherent in combinations of these elements.

the body

Basic body elements include:

Body parts —outer parts, such as head, shoulders, rib cage, hips, back, arms, hands, legs, and feet; and inner parts, such as heart, lungs, muscles, bones, and joints.

Body moves —such as stretching and bending, twisting and circling, rising and collapsing, swinging, swaying, and shaking.

There are numerous ways to categorize body parts and body moves. I have simply listed those with which I work.

The body is a marvelous instrument. It is fascinating to discover which parts can do which moves—to discover both the function of the body and the poetry of its use!

The third basic body element is *steps*. Because people have two feet, they can use them rhythmically and spatially to form eight basic steps. These are called *locomotor steps* because they carry the body from one place to another. They are:

walk: a transfer from one foot to the other on the ground
run: a transfer from one foot to the other off the ground
leap: an extended run
jump: taking off and landing on both feet
hop: taking off and landing on the same foot
skip: a step hop with an uneven beat
gallop: a run with an uneven beat, accent up
slide: a walk with an uneven beat, accent down, lead foot gliding

For teaching purposes, these steps can be organized as follows:

walk (and *run* and *leap*): transfer of weight from one foot to the other
jump: elevation on two feet
hop: elevation on one foot

Skip, gallop, and slide are variations or combinations of these three basic modes of locomotion.

So you can remember the three basics as the familiar hop, step, and jump that make up a standard track event.

space

Even when people are not moving, their bodies are making *shapes* in space, at a certain *level*. When they move, each move has *direction, size, focus,* a *place,* and a *pathway.* These are elements of space.

force

All movement can be altered by changes in force, depending on the *attack* (sharp or smooth), the *weight* (heavy or light), the *strength* (tight or loose), and the *flow* (free flowing, bound, or in balance). These are elements of force.

time

Movements have an underlying *beat* or pulse. They may have an *accent*. (Although accent is actually a force factor, it is so associated with time, through music, that it is here considered a time factor.) Movements always have a *speed* (fast or slow), and a *duration* (long or short). A combination of these elements of time produces a rhythmic *pattern*.

These basic elements comprise the world of dance. Thorough knowledge of the basics is essential to anyone contemplating the teaching of dance.

Once a teacher has a clear view of what is to be presented, the next step is determining how to present or structure it. Over the years I have developed my own model, and I present its structure and some sample lessons in this book. To show how these basic elements may be explored within this structure—with joy, involvement, and challenge for the personal and artistic growth of children—is the objective of this text.

THE IMPORTANCE OF CREATIVE DANCE

Creative dance is unique. It is the only activity in which physical movement is used nonfunctionally and as a personal expression. Children find a fulfillment through dance that can be realized through no other discipline, because dance simultaneously involves the inner being and the physical body. In dancing, children are not concerned with a game, an object, or even another person; their concentration and awareness are fixed on the act of moving.

Because of this focus, children discover a great deal about their bodies, minds, language, thoughts, imagination, and ideas through creative dance. They learn what the body can do, how they are put together, what strength and energy they have. They simultaneously leap and feel what it is like to leap. Besides becoming aware of themselves, they become aware of time, rhythm (patterns in time), and tempo. They become aware of space, direction, size, and level.

Dance experience teaches children both awareness and control of movement. They use these skills in games, sports, and everyday living. This heightened perception can be extended to the other arts. They may discover that the elements of dance are present in painting, music, and literature, and this awareness can help them appreciate line, design, mass, and shape in painting; melody, harmony, rhythm, and phrasing in music; and imagery and flow in literature. They learn how to "speak" through their bodies and so become aware of body language and its relation to words.

It is important for all children to be aware of themselves as growing, changing beings. Movement as creative expression plays an important part in life, building self-image, self-awareness, and self-direction. This *self* is not only the body, not only the mind, not only the feelings—it is all of the child. Awareness of self is of primary importance to difficult children, withdrawn children, exceptional children—all children. Creative dance leads children to deal with themselves. It is a clearly defined body of knowledge, in that it deals with elements that can be explored, learned, managed, and used. In other words, creative dance is a discipline for dealing with the self.

In addition, the experience of free large body movements during part of the school day has been shown to benefit children's ability to concentrate on "mental" subjects. Dance can, of course, be related to mathematics, social studies, language, and science; often it takes only a question or two from the teacher to start the children making the connections: "What is there in nature that uses its whole back to move through space?" "Can you skip sadly? Merrily? What other adverbs tell how you skip?" "Can you move in the shape of a triangle?" "Can you clap in threes?"

Movement for some reason seems to set the brain working. People find that, when they are under stress, they want to move. Movement is closely connected with the mind and the spirit. It is inherent in any kind of growth activity. The act of growing *is* movement. Mentally, spiritually, and physically, children need to move—a lot.

In each school day there should be a time when the children move freely and a time when they are guided in their movement. They should enlarge their movement vocabulary and increase their skill. Children improve their physical capacity to move simply by moving. Even without definite exercises and training programs, the child will increase in endurance, control, freedom, extension, balance, and rhythm through moving individually with complete involvement. The need to move makes children improve their ability to move. The teacher's role is to keep challenging them to stimulate and fulfill this need. The overall purpose is to open up movement as a means of expression.

Creative dance fosters the expressive capacities of the child. A painter uses canvas and colors. A musician uses an instrument and sound. A dancer uses his or her body and space, so that dance becomes a total personal expression—body, mind, and spirit engaged in a nonfunctional expression and communication of self. In no other area can this kind of expression be developed.

Children learn to hop, gallop, and skip by moving and experimenting, not by being taught. Because dance is so important to the physical and artistic growth of children, and because they grow by doing, the teacher has an obligation to present opportunities for this experimentation and growth. The ability to lead or guide is here more important than the ability to dance.

As a classroom teacher, you can lead the children in creative dance sessions. If you decide to try, you are in for a great adventure. With a regular program of dance, you can watch the children grow. You will see two things that tell you the children are on the way to growth: *joy* and *involvement.*

Most children grow up thinking that dance is a combination of steps that have to be learned. They are surprised and delighted to find that this is not so. Their faces and their bodies show joy. Their movement is abandoned, wild, free, but expressive and experimental. Their minds, their bodies, and their souls are completely involved in their movement.

Adults often say, "Dance is better than therapy." If the children knew about therapy, they would probably agree. In dance they can release their nerves from classroom tension, they can vent anger, they can express feelings of softness and calmness that they fear to show socially, they can use fantasy and imagination artistically. How great it is for them to learn that imagination is not just an escape or childish habit!

You may think that "free dancing" (see page 44) will be too embarrassing for a class. But children need and want to dance so badly they will ask for free dancing at each class, and they will usually be completely spent after a free dance period. This freedom can be used successfully and with self-assurance, however, only after preliminary exploration and learning of the elements of dance. Then what a wonderful gift the children have for the rest of their lives: the knowledge that they dance!

The children's perceptions of life, of technology, of themselves grow through dance training. They see the elements of dance in the world and find they can relate to and communicate about what they see and hear and feel. They develop and use their kinesthetic sense. They know their size, their strength, their timing; they are aware of movement control and flow. They can speak "body language" and can read it in others.

Many elementary schools have an athletic program, but no dance is included. Many have an art program, but dance is not included. Many have a music program, but movement is not included. In athletics, movement is functional. A ball must be caught or kicked, a person must be dodged. In calisthenics or exercises, flexibility, control, strength, and stretch are sought. Why not use that strength, coordination, and control in an experimental way that lets the child relate inner self to outer body, so that they are not two parts but the self as one whole being? In music, why not let children sway or swing to different rhythms, change level or direction with different phrases? In art, why not let children paint to music on paper big enough so that the body has to move? Why not have children make the shapes that they see using their bodies as well as their brushes?

Dance is closely related to these activities, but still it is unique. It is the only field in which art and activity simultaneously involve the individual, and so it is necessary for a total education. The craft, skill, and knowledge resulting from a study of dance constitute a distinct and separate field.

Physical education teachers, art teachers, music teachers, and classroom teachers all can teach creative dance because they are first of all teachers. Any teacher who is a creative teacher can teach creative dance. I hope that, after reading of my successes and failures, you will use the goals and the structure presented here to try creative dance with your class.

This kind of dance does not need storytelling, gimmicks, or special stimuli to motivate the children. It is both intriguing enough and important enough to be something they want to do. You can learn to ask the right questions and to lead in the right direction so that the children discover for themselves the experience of dance. Just as children experiment with the nature of building blocks (weight, thickness, size, and shape), they can explore the elements of dance (body, space, force, and time).

All children should dance sometime, someplace, every day—even if it is simply by leaping over puddles on their way home from school. One day a child told me he really had to leap over a puddle on the way home the day before. Next time the class met, we experimented with the many ways there are to go over a puddle. We could leap over it, hop over it, jump over it, walk over it. We could do all these things backwards, or sidewards. We could leap high and look down into it or look up as we went over it. We could turn as we crossed it. Your children will find all kinds of ways to go over a puddle that you may never have thought of!

Children love to leap and jump. Why not let them? Why not teach them to go further and further until they can use the force and rhythm of their bodies and the space around them in any and all possible ways? This is what dance is all about. You can teach them by suggestions and questions, by challenging them, and by structuring their ideas. You need no previous dance training. Even in a classroom crowded with desks and chairs, it is possible to do some dancing; but why not provide open space and at least some time each day for the children to dance? You do not have to be a dancer; you are a teacher. You just have to know your goals; (1) to teach the elements of dance, and (2) to structure that teaching so the children can experiment and grow.

THE GOAL

The goal of creative dance is to lead the children to creative use of the elements of dance. First they explore and experiment. Next they understand and control. Finally they use the elements.

The craft of dance may be compared to the tools children learn to use or the words they learn to speak. When children use these elements for their own creative expression, that is creative dance: they have made the connection between the inner being and the language of movement.

In order to reach this goal, in order for learning to take place, there must be a structured lesson plan. Each lesson (1) presents an element, (2) gives the children an opportunity for experimentation, and (3) requires the children to use the element in a simple form.

The elements overlap and cannot be dealt with singly, but in each lesson one particular element should be stressed so that the children know where to focus their attention. Understanding and use of that particular element becomes the goal for the day.

Don't forget to tell the children what is happening. Tell them what they will learn; tell them what they are learning; and then tell them what they have learned. Often we teachers have the goals clearly in mind, but we forget to communicate them to the children.

PITFALLS AND POINTERS

Once you know the elements of dance and have a structure for the lessons, you can learn to teach creative dance to children by experimentation—by trial and error. When things are not going well, or when the children seem to need a change, you can run to another part of the room and start the next challenge from there, or say, "Let's all come sit by the record player," or "Everyone come to the black line," or "Come sit by me."

Children need not line up or stand in formation in order to learn. They need not always be quiet. When I first started teaching, I neglected to give the children time to express verbally how they felt about moving. I wanted them to work out my ideas, not theirs, and I wanted the class to proceed as I had planned. I was not really free because I was afraid there would be noise and bedlam. I was afraid that if I laughed and played with the children I would lose control. Now I realize that control of the class comes from the structure, and within the structure there can be ease and freedom. Control is in the discipline of dance itself. Dancers do not bother each other or bump into each other; dancers use their bodies to dodge collisions and move around easily in crowded places. Children can learn this self-control.

Children like to be watched. How often do they say, "watch me"? But sometimes they are embarrassed to move freely in front of watchers. It is important to keep the class comfortable, free, and individualized. Experiment to resolve difficulties in this area.

You might give the children a smaller-group experience by dividing the class in half and having each group watch the other. Stress the fact that there is no right or wrong. The children will learn not to laugh at each other, to concentrate, to see the good things that others are doing, and to comment on them.

Call out the name of each child sometime during the session to let each one know you see him or her. Comment on a good shape, a use of strong muscles, the level, or whatever the child seems to be doing well.

At the end of class, have each child do a "good-bye dance" (see page 48). During this one-at-a-time ending, the child knows you are watching only her or him. The line of children moves fast, especially at the beginning of the term when their dances may be nothing more than an embarrassed walk from one side of the room to the other. As the term progresses, so do the good-bye dances. Use this opportunity to challenge the children individually ("Can you turn as you hop like that?") or to give them individual support ("You thought of hopping backwards. How interesting!") You will find the right combination of total group, small group, and individual activities for your particular class.

Many teachers use action songs to teach children rhythm and coordination. Some have the children skip or march to music. How much more fun it can be to have the children discover tempo by moving to their own heartbeats. Or they can skip as slowly as is humanly possible and then as fast as is humanly possible. Next they can accelerate and retard. Finally, they can march or skip to all kinds of music. Children can learn accent and phrasing by changing direction, level, or shape with musical phrases. They then are involved in discovering their own rhythm and controlling it.

Many good dancers fail at creative dance teaching because they are not sure of the goal. They are used to physical goals such as teaching the class to do a combination of steps. Not knowing what the goals in creative dance are and what body of knowledge is to be taught, they tend to confuse freedom with creativity. Their idea of teaching creatively is to suggest that the class move like elephants, butterflies, and so on. Some music is played, and the children, not knowing where to begin, giggle, and withdraw.

A well-intentioned teacher once asked her children to move to the music in any way they wanted to. This is quite an advanced assignment for most elementary children. Because they don't know the vocabulary, they are conscious of not knowing what to do. A few structured lessons giving them the vocabulary of dance and allowing them to learn what that vocabulary feels like would provide the security they need to do such an assignment.

I once watched a creative person encourage her children to move with hula hoops. She demonstrated some shapes and movements they might do, and asked, "What else can you do?" After a few minutes, one child started to hula with the hoop. Soon the rest followed. The teacher was at a loss what to do, so she collected the hoops and went on with something else. This teacher needed to prepare a structure. She could have asked her children for a shape at a low level, a shape at a middle level, and a shape at high level. Then she could have asked them to connect these shapes by movement. She might have asked how slowly they could keep the hoop moving, and how fast. She might have asked what steps they could do while moving the hoop. In other words, by using a structure based on the elements of dance, she could have led the children to discover their own capabilities with the hoop. Without a structure, without the vocabulary of the elements, they thought of only one way to move.

Some teachers tell or read stories with dramatic inflection and then have the children respond in action. This is fine as far as it goes, but is only a small part of the whole picture. Dance is a broad and deep subject. The art of communicating an action by dramatic or pantomimic gesture is only part of communicative movement and is quite separate from creative dance.

One book for elementary teachers contains a story to be danced by the children. The story is fine. (Almost any story is fine.) The children are to pretend they are on a journey where they see animals, which they are to imitate. Then the wind comes, a storm blows up, and so on. This is not creative on the children's part; it is imitative. It could be made creative by taking only a part of the story, say the animals, and working on that alone: "Show me the shape of your animal. How does it walk? How do its muscles move? Does it ever walk backwards?" Most children will go down on their hands and knees. Sometimes neither children nor teachers realize that being on all fours limits people. Free the children from this limitation. "Can you show me that kind of movement at a high level? At a middle level? How does your animal sleep? How does it spring into action?"

In other words, go deeper into the movement until the children make the movement their own interpretations of that animal. Dance should give the *feeling* of the animal rather than simply an imitation of one. The great deer dance of Mexico is a wonderful example of an animal dance. In watching it, we feel the presence of a deer—its quick, light, rhythmic step, its bounding freedom, its sharp stops of alertness, and finally its vulnerability and death. The dancer is expressing feelings shared with the deer, not just imitating the action of the animal.

Recently I watched a teacher work with fourth grade boys and girls. She told a story of cowboys and bucking broncos, while they danced it. When the cowboys were riding the range, the children did a lot of wild galloping and laughing. I don't think any of them thought they were dancing; they thought they were playing. In the creative dance situation, children should be taught the names of the elements of dance. How can they know what they are learning if they are not told where to concentrate? If they had learned the eight basic steps (walk, run, leap, jump, hop, gallop, skip, slide), the cowboys could have been asked to use another step to show riding. They could have been asked to do a slow-motion movie of riding the range.

Freedom does not help creativity; discipline and structure do. Use the elements to force the children to change and to add variety. Dance is a craft; children need to know that it has certain basic elements, which are named and used. Sometimes it helps to write on the board what the children have learned each day so that they see their growth and do not think of all that action as merely play. They need to talk about movement, so they should know movement terminology. Comments from other students on the bucking broncos might have been, "He didn't concentrate," "They needed more change of level," "There was no variety," "The tempo was the same all the time and so were the shapes of the riders."

It is easy to see the mistakes of others, isn't it? Most failures seem to occur when the teacher does not have the goal clearly in mind and does not know what specific thing is to be learned that particular day—in other words, when preparation or structure is lacking.

If you have been working with children, you will probably agree that every day is not a good day; or, to phrase it better, good days come in different ways, and sometimes not in *your* way. For example, one day my preschoolers began to run around the room in the middle of class. They didn't stop, and I thought, "What should I do now?" I sat down and watched them. This seemed to give them a spurt of energy, and even those who thought before that they shouldn't be running now joined the crowd. Soon they grew tired and all came to sit beside me, breathless. They were smiling, and I couldn't help but smile too. I was so pleased that they had come to sit down and be my class once more! We all were in a great mood then, and the class went on.

It is good not to be too upset by noise and movement. The children know that what you have in store for them is going to be fun. Dance is challenging, exciting, meaningful—and personal. You can't beat all that!

Ask the children to remove their shoes and socks. This makes them aware that dance is something different. Being barefoot keeps them from sliding, cuts down on the noise, prevents them from hurting each other if they kick by mistake, and promotes freer use of the feet, ankles, and legs. If you are in a situation where you can ask the children to wear special clothing, I would suggest gym suits, bathing suits, leotards, shorts, or long pants. Clothes affect the way people move and feel about themselves. You will promote greater attention, involvement, and growth if the children remember that on dance days they wear certain clothes. Another reason for special dance clothes or old clothes is that the children tend to get dirty from the floor while dancing. However, *some* dance is better than no dance, so have them dance even if they are in skirts and boots!

Some children like to leave on their socks. I tell those children to leave their shoes on too. Socks are terribly slippery; shoes give some traction. I also tell them that no dancer ever dances in stocking feet—either bare feet or shoes. Most children sooner or later take off their shoes and socks because they want to. One of my students would not take off her shoes for a year. Suddenly, this year, she decided to take them off for dance. None of us knows why.

The floor must be clean. In many classes I have a broom committee, composed of students, to check the floor each day. The children love to do this.

The older children usually laugh a lot the first few days of dance. Some children laugh so loudly and so long at just making shapes that I never cease to be amazed. I usually tell them, "I know how crazy it is, and we'll be doing even crazier things, but we'll never get past shapes if you can't hear me." I try once more, and if they continue to giggle, as they usually do, I change quickly to "stop and go" (see lesson 2) and then

Getting ready

move onto "steps" (see lesson 4). After that I end the session. The next time I begin with shapes again. Gradually they become serious, and the sessions can be accomplished with the feeling of fun still in the air.

I frequently jump from lesson to lesson within a session, when necessary, rather than continuing an unsuccessful course. I also switch the students from moving in a group to moving one at a time or have them come to a different place in the room. This helps to keep things active and interesting. It is not the nature of children to stand still, sit still, or remain in formation.

There will be all kinds of noise in the class: laughter, talking, heavy feet, clapping, who knows what else? So *you* must have a *greater noise*. *Greater* does not necessarily mean *louder,* although this sometimes helps; it means your noise must command respect. Your drum or your hands or your voice must demand what you want it to demand. My voice demands that their voices cease, my drum demands movement, and when my drum stops, the silence demands a shape.

It is often a good idea to have some children play drums, sticks, or maracas while others move. But every teacher needs a controlling noisemaker. In leading any kind of movement in a group situation, it is important to be able to start and stop the movement. I use my *voice* as my noisemaker. I do not permit the children to speak vocally while they are moving, because I want to talk. I like to use my voice to ask challenging questions, to stimulate their imaginations, and to bring the movement to an end.

Music (live or recorded) can be a noisemaker. I use music during a class as I would a drum or my voice—to start and stop the movement and to add color, feeling, challenge. Notice that I have not said anything about rhythm. Speaking or beating a drum in rhythm with movement is a difficult thing to do. I think the noisemaker should be dramatic rather than musical or rhythmic, so that teachers who feel ill at ease rhythmically will have one less worry.

I do not dance in my classes. I talk, beat the drum, play records, sit on the floor, dash to another corner, mingle. I do lots of moving around, but no dancing. That is why I am convinced that a nondancer can do the job.

It is well known that children study better when their bodies are free. It is recognized that movement promotes learning. Body and mind are inseparable, and we must educate the whole person, the "together" person. Dance is a must in the elementary school. *You* can teach it!

WHAT TO EXPECT

What can you expect from your class in dance? It depends on the age of the children.

Four- and five-year-olds can isolate parts of their bodies, do all the body moves, and do most of the steps (walk, run, leap, jump, hop, gallop, skip, slide). Galloping is usually the favorite step, with hopping and jumping close behind. Although some skip at four, skipping comes slowly to others. Most children can skip by the time they are six. Leaping, as differentiated from running, and sideward sliding are skills learned at four and five.

Kindergartners love making shapes. They understand level, direction, and size, but their understanding of place, pathways, and focus may not be as developed. They can explore force factors in the extremes, such as sharp—smooth, heavy—light, and tight—loose. Control over the time factors of beat, speed, and accent is often evident, and movement is often related to sound, but these skills are usually developed later. However, little ones love working with fast and slow, and they often show definite rhythmic skill.

Six- to eight-year-olds are more skillful in their control of all these factors, and are able to remember and repeat their dance movements. They relate to time and space with more understanding.

Nine- to twelve-year-olds can control their moves with greater

Making shapes on the first day

physical ability. With their heightened mental awareness, they can explore in depth all the elements of dance in all facets. They enjoy group work because of their social development and their space—time awareness, and they can readily experiment with relationships.

What factors will tell you whether you are on the right track? *Expression.* The children will tell you verbally how they feel. They will show you in movement how they feel. By watching and listening you will learn whether they are using their capacities to the fullest, whether they are enjoying the sessions, and whether they are learning the elements of dance. When you enjoy watching them perform, when you see them make unusual and interesting shapes, when you see them do movements that excite you by their physical skill or personal conviction, then you will know you have succeeded in reaching the children.

I find that the main challenge and the main key in reaching them is the same for all ages: *variety.* Every person must work within his or her own capabilities, and the sign of growth is something new, something different for each.

Always ask for variety. Kindergartners can begin in a shape, do some movements that have variety, and make an ending shape. All children can gallop around the room; with your challenge, they can progress to galloping a few times, then changing to floor level for some shapes, and then rising to do some jumps.

For a five-year-old, then, variety might be adding a jump after some gallops. For a six- to eight-year-old it might be moving very lightly after a period of moving rather heavily. For a nine- to twelve-year-old it might mean adding a stop or some isolated movement of a body part to the usual full body movement, or it might be changing a characteristic tempo.

Of course, age characteristics overlap. Like the twelve-year-old, the five-year-old may change a characteristic tempo. That is growth! For guideposts along the way to involvement and growth, look and listen for expression and variety.

Gradually over the years I have become aware of the detrimental influence of using imagery, imitation, and ideas to teach dance. At the outset I easily accepted and used all the wonderful stimuli for dance: "Everyone be a seed, and show me the flowers growing"; "Let me see the wild horses galloping"; "Show me the ice cream melting." After teaching this way for a while, I wondered why the children could compose only dances that told stories. I saw only pantomimic movement, and, whether they danced my ideas or theirs, all the dances were literary, were emotional, or pretended something; all were fantasy. I couldn't understand what had gone wrong. Why couldn't my children make dances that were *dances?* Why weren't they involved in the *movement* possibilities of an idea, rather than only the idea itself? Then I realized that ideas were exactly what they had been taught: I had taught them to be "like" something, rather than to dance as human beings.

How I wish I could call back all those classes and start them anew! I thought I had been teaching dance, but I had been merely skirting the art, always relating it to something it was not. I had fallen into a series of doll dances, witch dances, storm dances, dances based on animal movement, dances based on gesture. I had pored over every new book that was written to glean new ideas that could inspire and motivate the children to dance.

Something was wrong, and the children's program of fights, women cleaning house, hunters and turkeys, dolls coming alive, boats, kites, chickens, and airplanes brought the difficulty into focus. The wonderful world of *dance* had hardly been explored.

Then I began to talk only in terms of movement, with no imagery at all. It was just as exciting to slash the arms through the air and jab with the knees as it was to be wild horses, and the result was that the children learned about dance movement and about their own bodies. It was real, not pretense. We could fantasize about Mr. Knee or Ms. Elbow rising in space, and it produced far more learning about dance than witches leaping. Dance is not *about* something. Dance *is* something.

In teaching dance to children, it is sometimes easy to forget this. I talked about being horses, dolls, machines, and wind instead of movement, space, force, and time. Then I wondered why the children responded by pretending rather than by dancing. Revelation comes with the discovery that dance teaching must be involved primarily with movement education, exploration, and development. Only after the children learn the scope of dance and the vocabulary of the elements, only after they have experimented with the craft of dance can they relate dance to other areas through imagery. This relating is a second step.

This does not preclude using images to *lead to* the understanding of movement. If the movement itself is of first importance when you say, "Make your body round like an orange," "Stretch thin and tall like an arrow," "Gallop like a wild horse," "Leap over a huge puddle," or "Feel strong force from inside and strike out as in anger," such words can be effective. Images that *arise from* a movement can also be used effectively, for example, when you say, "What moves like that?" Such passing use of imagery that leads to or arises from movement is acceptable and, in fact, can help in the teaching of dance.

What does not help, and what is not acceptable, at least in the first steps of teaching creative dance, is dancing *about* anger, oranges, arrows, or horses. Dancing about things can be a stumbling block unless and until the basic elements have been grasped.

When you put aside all the gimmicks and ideas, you can see dance as an entity. You can present that entity clearly to the children, and they can grasp it easily. When it becomes theirs through exploration, they can use it as a personal expression. Later they will see the relationship of stories, designs, music, and feelings. Then they will be able to dance *about* all kinds of ideas because they will have learned the nature and province of dance.

At that later date, when the children dance about wild horses, the freedom and wildness will appear in individual ways, because each child will relate her or his own dance experience and capacity for movement to the idea. One may choose not only to gallop but also to leap and to jump. Another may elect to make quick changes in tempo or may choose to roll and stretch slowly. A third may make twisted pathways with great force or prance lightly with carefree turns. Each choice will be individual because each child will be using the elements of dance in a personal way.

"Show wildness, freedom, and horselike movement"—that is a big order for children. How can they possibly attempt it and truly be choosing and directing their own movements unless they have had experience with the elements of movement first? Talk about movement first and horses second. Elements are the first step; imagery and ideas the second step.

Thus, in the use of imagery there are three phases:

1. Images that lead to movement: "Make your back round like an orange."

2. Images that arise from movement: "You're in a round shape. What else do you know that's round?"

3. Images as a basis for movement: "What kind of movement might an orange do?"

images that lead to movement

While students are experimenting with the craft of dance, it is sometimes helpful to relate the movements they are doing to things outside the body. They "sway like a branch in the wind," "creep like a lion," "grow like a flower," or "jump like popcorn." This use of imagery can be limiting, however, unless the focus is kept on the movement rather than on the image.

The teacher who says, "Jump like popcorn," must also say, "Now jump like a firecracker," "Now jump like a kangaroo," "Now jump like a slow-motion film." It must be clear that the thing to be explored is the jumping, with its various time, space, and force possibilities: jump lightly, using small space; jump suddenly and sharply; jump heavily, using a large space; jump slowly. The assignment must be a jumping dance, not a dance about popcorn. The focus and intent must remain on the elements of dance. If the focus is placed on the image—popcorn— you'll find your children pretending they are popcorn, instead of dancing. They might even pick at each other and pretend to eat!

They may discover many ways of jumping like popcorn. They may do small "jumps" with their shoulders, their backs, or their legs. They may get larger and larger. They may cover space and use directions. The trouble is, they may not.

With children, imagery is very strong, and it can limit their exploration. Older children may be more experimental in finding ways to use the elements of movement in a popcorn dance, but smaller children will think more about the popcorn than about the jumping.

Why take the chance that they may not develop the idea of jumping? Why not make sure by challenging them to make a jumping dance? Going from a small to a large shape with sharp light jumps is more educational and challenging than pretending to be popcorn. Talk in dance language and not in image language. Then the children will talk and think and act in dance, and they will develop dance skill and knowledge.

I used to teach a collapse by the image of ice cream melting. "Show me the shape of a huge scoop of ice cream. Now let it melt. What kind of movement is that? How does your body feel? How much force is there? What is the direction?" Then I would transfer this understanding of the movement to other actions: "Can you walk with that same light, smooth flow gradually changing levels?"

What a waste of time! Now I say, "Show me a collapse." They all know this word (or, if they don't, I teach them), and it is a movement word. Then: "How slowly can you collapse? Can you collapse and not change level? Can you walk with a collapsed shape? Can you walk and collapse at the same time?" Then, without trying to think of an association or image, I have them work on a dance that involves collapsing movement and its counterpart, rising.

In this way, the focus is on dance language and skill. If an image of ice cream or sadness or pain or dangling rope or Raggedy Ann helps momentarily, good! But the starting and ending point is collapse—a basic body move and the element for the day.

Children can see the goals and aims of dance class much more clearly when the teacher knows what she or he wants to teach. They will later dance from images more thoroughly, creatively, and beautifully when they discover for themselves the relationship of imagery to dance. They will become aware of the rhythm of tension and release in sports activities and stories; they will delight in shape and form in painting, in the direction and force of wind and water, in the changing shapes of human feeling.

In the meantime, each child will take great joy in direct awareness and control of his or her body in space and the ability to express and communicate through movement.

images that arise from movement

The second step in the use of imagery is to let an idea or image emerge from the movement. When a child likens a movement to something else, it can be a sign of growth. The child is aware of relatedness.

When a teacher asks, "What do you know that moves like that?" the answers sometimes are astounding. A lesson on bones made the children think of lightning and scissors; a lesson on breath elicited clouds and the ocean; and a lesson on muscles brought forth monsters and cement mixers. When a child's answer has no relationship to the movement or when the relationship is unclear, then the class can discuss the differences and thereby come to a closer understanding of the movement.

It is often good to stimulate the imagination in this way, and the children come up with fantastic ideas. Sometimes you'll want to go right on to something else; at other times you may want to follow through with one or two ideas that seem most relevant and stimulating to the children. In that case, you can structure the idea through questions just as you would if the idea came before the movement—as in the third phase of imagery. (Structuring ideas or images is discussed at length in the chapter on method.) The first and second phases are spontaneous and may be helpful; they arise simultaneously with study of the elements of dance. The third phase is different.

imagery as a basis for dance

First, let me describe a few failures: One day the children ran to me before class saying they wanted to dance about a Christmas tree coming alive. They wanted to work it out themselves and show it to me as a surprise. It turned out to be a pantomime of children decorating a tree and then making astounded shapes at seeing it move.

Why didn't they think in dance terms? Why did they fall into drama and skit-making? I had noticed my children calling their dances "plays." Other teachers called them "sketches." Why not dances?

The probable answer is that children and adults alike still think of dance in terms of entertainment. It must be steps done to music. Movement from within the body that does not always involve steps is still relatively new to many people. Movement as communication and movement as art are unfamiliar. How, then, can children be expected to call what they create a "dance"?

If dance teachers allow or lead the children to make dances from ideas before they conceive of what dance is, then they should not be surprised to get something other than dance in return.

I returned to my Christmas tree dancers the following week armed with a chart showing them what dance elements they had learned. We reviewed body moves and steps, levels, directions, size, force, and time.

Then we made simple combinations of a body move (collapse) with a step (skip), or a size (small) with a move (twist) or a step (gallop). They found that some combinations were possible and some were not. They were highly stimulated by the challenge and kept running back to my chart to check on other combinations.

Then I had them each choose one of the following elements: time (fast and slow), force (sharp and smooth), or size (big and little). They were allowed to use any body moves, any directions, any levels, and any steps, but they were challenged to find as many movements as they could and to perform them in their chosen category, either fast and slow, big and little, or sharp and smooth.

Then I asked them to feel whether their movements would more likely fit a person or a thing around the tree. Some decided they were children, some were toys. When we finally arranged the dance, there was a real concentration on moving with contrast, not pretending. It was dancing, not pantomiming.

Until we did the complete review, they really had not swallowed and digested what I had been teaching. I should have stressed their creative use of the elements earlier, and I should have directed their development of ideas by teaching them to think in movement terms. I had only presented the elements to them, and had not shown them how to use elements in a way that would be creative.

Dance and its craft must be understood first. If children are allowed to create from an idea too soon, as mine did with their Christmas tree dance, they do not have enough command or skill in using the tools of dance—the elements—and so cannot be successful. They will feel they are playing, not accomplishing or constructing or growing. Until they know the language of dance, how can they help but fall into drama or pantomime?

I had a similar experience with another class. They wanted to dance about death. We discussed the kinds of movements people do when someone dies—around the bedside, at the church, at the grave. We also discussed the kinds of feelings an individual might have that could be expressed in movement. The class divided into groups. One group was to do a dance of excited frenzy at the home, the next planned to do a funeral march, and the third, a church scene.

The dance was never realized. When they thought of church, they could think only of praying. The marchers could only march, and the excited family thought only of running to tell the neighbors. Each action they thought of was pantomimic. We could have put the actions together to form a pantomime story, but it would not have been a dance because the actions or movements were concerned with function rather than expression.

If I, as the teacher, had discussed the idea in terms of the elements of dance, I think we would have had success. I should have asked, "What kind of body shapes do people assume when death is at hand? What kind of focus? What kind of force? What tempo? Show me some sad or grief-stricken shapes. In what direction would the movement go?" By using movement words, I should have made clear the relationship of the idea to dance.

We might have divided into three groups again; this time the first would have done moves changing levels, the second locomotor movements, and the third contrasting types of force (perhaps sharp and piercing, weak and smooth). Their knowledge of church, funerals, and the bedside would have supported their movement ideas but would not have submerged them. Such a series of questions and such a structure would have given the children a clear understanding of how to go about creating a dance from an idea.

Great dancers can communicate depths of feeling through movement. In their work the craft and the feeling become one. In order to approach this oneness, dancers must begin at the beginning. They must first learn what the body can do, and how it can be done. Art grows from exploration, experimentation, and creative use of its elements.

It is important, therefore, to work with the basic craft of dance first. Second, let ideas arise from the movement so that the children become aware of the kinds of ideas that are suitable to dance.

Third, after the basics have been established and explored, ideas and images can be presented as problems or assignments. If this is done too soon, children tend to express the ideas dramatically, through pantomime, because they are familiar with movement as describing functional or verbal actions. When they become familiar with movement as a distinct and separate area of expression, not just an interpreter for dramatic action, then they will know dance. When they know how to work with the elements of the art, they can attempt to build a dance *about* an idea or image. They will, of course, need your guidance in structuring their ideas.

In the next chapter, on method, I discuss structuring such an idea or image into a dance. However, first things first! I start with the elements and structuring the elements. Then I will go on to structuring an idea.

2

The Method

THE ELEMENTS

This may be the shortest section in the book, but it is the most important. The elements of dance, the tools of the craft, are basic to life. You already know them, although you probably have not organized them in this particular way.

Study and memorize them. Think about how they are part of your daily life. Each time you move you use the elements. You lower your level as you step into the bath tub, you stretch to reach for a jar on a high shelf, you use force to raise a stubborn window and to flick crumbs from the table. You twist to talk to the person behind you. You shake your head. You run for the bus.

You must become so conscious of the elements and so familiar with them that you can call upon them instantly as you teach. You will need them at the back of your head—or at your fingertips (whichever place suits you best). Make them part of you now.

ELEMENTS OF DANCE

Body	Body parts	Inner: muscles, bones, joints, heart, lungs (breath)
		Outer: head, shoulders, arms, hands, back, rib cage, hips, legs, feet
	Body moves	Stretch, bend, twist, circle, rise, collapse, swing, sway, shake
	Steps	Walk, run, leap, hop, jump, gallop, skip, slide
Space	Shape	Body design in space
	Level	High, middle, low
	Direction	Forward, backward, sideward, turning
	Size	Big, little
	Place	On the spot, through space
	Focus	Direction of gaze
	Pathway	Curved, straight
Force	Attack	Sharp, smooth
	Weight	Heavy, light
	Strength	Tight, loose
	Flow	Free-flowing, bound, or balanced
Time	Beat	Underlying pulse
	Tempo	Fast, slow
	Accent	Force
	Duration	Long, short
	Pattern	Combinations

The structure of a lesson has three steps:

1. Present the element you want to teach

2. Have the children explore its possibilities

3. Give it form

The method used should be one of questions and challenges. The children need to learn from the inside out. They need to find out for themselves what their bodies can do. So, remember: even in the simplest tasks, ask them, don't show them.

presentation

In presenting the element to be learned, first use any visual aid, words, materials, or gimmicks that make clear what it is the children are to learn. For a lesson on swinging, you might bring a pendulum made of a string and a weight or a yo-yo. Rubber bands, feathers, soft clay, plastic bags, and the like can help clarify movement characteristics such as stretch and collapse, lightness and heaviness, change in size, and change in tempo. Windows, clocks, flags, and pictures have shapes, and the pathways of their designs can be reflected in movement.

Next, ask the class "how," "what," and "where." In the lesson on swinging, the questions might be:

"How does the body swing?"

"What makes a swinging movement?"

"What parts of the body can swing?"

"Where does a swing go in space?"

Present, suggest, and define until they know what the element is. Have the children experiment by doing the movement first on the spot and then through space. Have them try it with different parts of their bodies. Have them try all the steps with the element. Have them try it at all levels and in all directions. Next have them experiment with its opposite. Have them change the speed and force of the move. In other words, challenge them to do the element in any and every possible way. This exploratory section of the lesson is perhaps the most important.

How does a teacher find the right questions to ask to make the exploration fruitful? You find questions, suggestions, and challenges by *crossing over* to another element and asking the children to perform the two elements together. I call this teaching method the *crossover* technique. If the element for the day is a *body part,* for example, find questions by crossing over to body moves and steps and to the remaining three elements: space, force, and time.

body steps: ask how this part can move while the feet do steps

space: have the children change shape, level, and direction with that part leading

force: have them try to make the movement of that part sharp and smooth, strong and light, tense and loose

time: ask them to move the part quickly, slowly, with an accent, in a pattern

An element is explored through the changed movement that is produced by combining or crossing it with other elements. Of course, it is impossible for any part of one element to be used without also using the other three elements, but, to simplify matters in teaching, first consider an element as a separate entity and then vary it by combining it with others.

Suppose the element to be explored is swinging movement. You have just introduced it by asking "how," "what," "where" questions. For your crossover questions, then, go right down the list of the elements:

Body

1. What body parts can swing?

2. What really swings—muscles? Bones? Joints?

3. Can you swing and bend? Swing and stretch? Swing and shake?

4. Can you swing while you skip? Gallop? Run?

Space

5. Find an upside-down shape. What can swing now?

6. Can you swing at a low level?

7. In how many directions can you swing?

8. Can you swing your focus? Can you change focus while you swing?

9. Can you use a swing to propel yourself through space?

10. Can you use a swing to make a curved path in space?

Force

11. Can a swing be sharp?

12. Can it be strong?

13. Can it be tense?

14. Show me a free-flowing swing and then sudden stillness.

15. Can you swing and find a new balance?

Time

16. Show me a swing with an even beat.

17. Show me an accent at the low part of the swing. Show me one at the crest.

18. How slowly can you swing?

19. Can you make a long swing and then some short ones?

20. Can you swing in an uneven pattern?

Another teacher might find a totally different set of questions. All teachers use the same elements, but each presents different challenges. It becomes your individual project to choose how you will use crossovers to stimulate the children to explore the same basic elements.

If you are working on breath movement, ask the children to breathe deeply to find how their bodies move as they breathe. Then have them extend that movement until they change levels, rising on the inhalation and sinking on the exhalation. Next, change the speed, using gasps. Then increase the force until the intake becomes a jump. Have them move around the room, through space, carrying themselves forward as they inhale and relaxing as they exhale. Challenge them to try gallops, skips, and leaps with a breath impulse. Finally, forget the actual breathing, and concentrate on the kind of movement it produces.

When the element to explore is fast movement, the children can discover which body parts can move fast, which moves and which steps can be done fast. Ask them, "What do you know that moves fast and low? Fast and sideward? Fast and small? Fast and sharp? Fast and light? Fast and free?" After you have tried combining two, try combining three, four, or five. Surprise them with a challenge to create a fast, high, light, small, sideward move. You see how interesting such exploration can become!

Use the crossover technique with any element. Try some examples now: look again at the table of elements on page 32. Choose one, and see what crossovers you find interesting. Start at the top of the list and try to form a question with each element. Your use of crossovers will be unique and individual. The questions you think of will be your own way of bringing dance experience to your children. Watch your ability grow as your memory and imagination are stimulated.

form

When you have asked every possible question, structure the children's learning into a simple form. They can choose particular movements, working alone, with a partner, or in groups. The form is

1. Starting shape
2. Varied movements selected from their explorations
3. Ending shape

Shape, movement, shape.

In order to make a phrase based on breath movement, for example, ask the children to choose and put together several ways to use breath movement. They can select moves from among those they have just explored. They may choose to do all the variations they can think of or to select moves that arise from an image. You begin by saying, "Ready, starting shape, begin." You might want to play music. When they have danced several different ways, then call out: "and make an ending shape." These dance studies are very short—perhaps fifteen or twenty seconds long.

When children first begin to put their movements into a form, they need to feel secure about the beginning and ending. Therefore, take plenty of time to look at their starting shapes. Comment on them before any movement begins. I tell the children they must look like dancers, not like ordinary people. Words such as "There is an interesting low shape," and "Look at that high twisted shape," help.

The middle part is the main part. Here the children should try for *variety* and *clarity*. You can help by reminding them, even while they are dancing, to include a change of level or movement through space (remembering the crossovers). Constantly challenge them to find new and different movements.

The ending is as important as the beginning. When they cannot think of anything different or more interesting to do, they must end. I tell my children that when they find they have done the same move four times, and they can't add something new, they should end. There must be variety or the dance will be boring and too long. They should hold the ending shape to show it is the end. In the early sessions, it is best for the teacher to bring the dance phrases to an end *sooner* than the children wish. This causes them to find variations sooner and is comforting to those who are less skilled.

Shape, movement, shape—this is their dance. After they have done one, comment and have the children repeat the dance phrase. There is no need for the children to memorize the movements; this is improvisation. When they repeat the dance, it may be completely different the second time. The beginning shape, the varied middle, and the ending shape will fill the need for stability and the sense of completing "a dance." When you feel that all are secure and have some movement to work with, divide the class in half and have the two groups watch each other.

What is important is that the children experiment with a particular kind of movement, using many other elements in combination with it. When they select and use some of these movements in a form, they are using their new awareness of the element in their own way. This is the goal.

Some children giggle and feel silly about performing in front of others or watching others perform. I tell them, "Hold your concentration." I comment favorably on those who can control their concentration and pay attention to what they are doing, whether it is dancing or observing. I keep the dances very, very short and the assignment very clear and highly structured. I keep the groups large enough so that if one or two children are having difficulty performing, they can hide in the group, and I am careful not to call attention to them. At their first sign of effort to control themselves and their movements, I compliment them. This gives the self-conscious child a feeling of some success and security. It is very important for the children to concentrate and keep their minds and bodies together to dance; often it is helpful to do some special exercises to build this skill and habit. Make concentration as important as moving. Try relaxation activities, yoga asanas, sensitivity and awareness sessions, and even games. All can help children control their concentration.

At the end of the session, ask *yourself* some questions (see also Evaluation, page 67): "Did we fully explore an element?" "Did they try movements they would not have tried without my questions?" "Did I challenge them to extend their ability?" "Did they select and use movements of their own choice at some point during the lesson?"

I hope your answer to each will be a resounding "yes".

STRUCTURING AN IDEA

You structure an idea in exactly the same way that you structure the children's work with the elements:

1. Present the idea
2. Have the children explore its possibilities
3. Give it form

presentation

The idea can be presented by you or the children. Question, discuss, and define it.

The crossover technique is again used to relate the image to movement. What movement possibilities are inherent in the idea? For example, when two of my girls wanted to dance as trees, they first found a starting shape. Then we crossed over to other elements of dance to find if these trees had twisted trunks, if they were high or low, if they were big or little, if they swayed lightly or strongly, if they shook, if they stretched, if they bent, if their branches made straight or curved pathways, and so on. The children were surprised at how much choice of movement there was—for trees! And we had not mentioned feeling words, only movement words.

There are three additional methods for expanding both the movement and the idea. One of these is *contrast*. When an eight-year-old wanted to dance about the winter wind, I asked the class first to move as a slow, gentle, summer breeze, then their moves grew into the fierce, frigid, fast, winter wind, and then they froze absolutely still. By using contrast, they made the winter wind movement stronger and gave the dance form.

Another method is *space control*. When a four-year-old asked to dance about reindeer, the class first experimented with how the head would feel with those long horns, and how those long legs would stretch and bend. Then they trotted and galloped over rooftops, only to return at last to the north pole to stretch their necks and legs once more before retiring. In other words, we used a sequence based on the element of space: stay in one spot, move through space, return to the spot.

A third way to help put a child's idea into movement is by *extension* of the idea. One twelve-year-old thought of toothpaste as an idea for dancing! Who could have been prepared for that? First the children did smooth, slow, long movements as the toothpaste itself. Then they moved as the tube, which gradually became either rolled up or crinkled out of shape. Then we extended the idea: the children became magical toothpaste that could slither out of the tube, around the room, and back into the tube.

In order to find movement for an idea, then, (1) relate the idea to dance by questions involving the elements (crossovers), and (2) use contrast, space control, and extension, to increase movement possibilities.

form

The third step in structuring an idea is to put the movements into a form: shape, movement, shape. The children select and organize their movements, enclosing them between a beginning shape and an ending shape.

Sometimes it is expedient to present, explore, and form an idea quickly just for fun and recreation. This is especially helpful with young children who have short attention spans and with older children on days when they feel hyperactive but not quite ready for exploration in depth.

One day, for example, while sitting on the floor with four- and five-year-olds, I said, "What shall we dance about today?"

They were quiet for a minute, and then one said, "A princess."

"Oh," I said, "and how does a princess move? How does she walk around her palace? How does she turn in that long beautiful dress?"

They began to walk and turn, looking very haughty. Then I said, "And what does this princess do besides walk around her palace?"

"Nothing," they said, "she just rests."

"Show me how the princess rests," I said. They began to take restful poses very slowly and elegantly.

"There she is," I said, "just resting. And then what happens?"

All were quiet for a moment, and then one shouted, "A witch comes in!"

"Oh," I said, "show me the shape of that witch." They all took very twisted, bent shapes. "Show me how that witch can move in that twisted bent shape. Can she hop? Can she jump? Without losing her witch's shape?" They tried and found they could hop and jump in their twisted, crooked shapes. "And what did the princess do when she saw the witch?"

"She screamed!" they said.

"How can you scream with your body? Show me." They showed me some marvelous screams. Some contracted every part of their bodies, some stretched and reached, some covered their mouths. "And what did she do then?"

"She ran."

"All the way over to this corner," I said. "And what did the witch do?"

"She went away." Off they all walked in their witch's shapes, and the dance was over.

I was thrilled with this little episode because it was as much a surprise and a challenge to me as it was to the children. I tried hard to use their ideas and not to lead them through ideas of mine. It kept me on my toes trying to relate everything they said to movement. It just happened that their story was full of movement ideas—and a variety of them. I can truly call it a dance and not a pantomime because the children moved in depth with each movement cue. The screams were not imitations of screaming, but had the force, size, and direction each child associated with a scream.

On another occasion, I asked a group of ten- and eleven-year-olds to write down an idea for a dance—an idea that had some movement in it. After reading and talking about each idea, developing and elaborating it verbally, I asked them to call out their favorites or those that they could remember most clearly. These were the ideas they chose: Mexican dance, swans, clowns, jumping beans, flowers on the moon, rainstorm, snakes, and butterflies. When I said that we would now dance each and every idea, they jumped and clapped with excitement.

"What do you know about Mexico?" I asked.

They answered, "Mexican Hat Dance," "Big skirts," "Men sitting under big hats," "Fiesta."

We decided to have a fiesta, and we would be the dancers. "Show me first what you can do at a low level with just your body and your arms under that big hat to this beat." I tried to sing and beat something sounding vaguely Mexican. "Now show me the rhythm with your feet." Then, "How can these Mexicans turn? How can they move around the room? Now show me an ending shape."

"Swans: who has actually seen a swan? What is their shape? How do they move through the water? How do they fly? How do they rest?"

"Clowns: what kinds of clowns are you?" I asked.

"We're clowns that make children laugh," they said.

"What kind of movement would make a child laugh?" On this, they were a little wild, so we ended rather quickly, but we were all laughing.

We went through the entire list in about ten or fifteen minutes.

I mention these two incidents because they made me realize the great joy and abandon with which children attack creative dance. Even in a brief session, if I helped by asking questions and structuring their ideas, much learning took place.

The ability to structure an idea so that learning can take place is the most important ability for leading creative dance. After "The Princess and the Witch," I realized that, had I not been able to structure their ideas for them, they might have rested forever in their palace. Something had to happen to make movement occur, so I asked a question. If they had not thought of something, I would have had to think of something. That is why I say structure is the teacher's responsibility. When the older children thought of Mexico, swans, clowns, and the rest, I had to ask questions that brought forth movement or shapes. Within the form, I structured the ideas using crossover questions. In effect, I asked:

1. What is the shape of the thing?
2. What kind of movement does it do?
3. What is the shape of the ending?

In other words, shape, movement, shape.

When we did snakes, if I had not forced them to change levels, we would have had snakes that could move only on the floor. But I had them extend the idea and imagine snakes moving upward through space. This brought a new dimension to the idea and challenged them to think in terms of movement rather than simply of imitating snakes. You have to get the children past simply pretending to be something—snakes, swans, clowns, or princesses. In order to do this, you must know what to ask and how to structure. You need not know how to do the movement yourself.

Many children can benefit greatly from a dance experience taught by the classroom teacher. Any teacher who really wants to do so can learn to be the encourager, the leader, the questioner, the challenger, the organizer. You need to know where you are going (the goal) and how to get there (the structure).

Remember, in the midst of all these words, that people dance primarily to express what cannot be expressed verbally. So all ideas and images are merely helpers through which the children become aware of themselves, of movement, of time, of space, and of energy, so that they can truly direct their bodies, dance their own ways, and express things that cannot be communicated in any other way.

SPECIAL DANCES

free dancing

In *free dance,* everyone dances at the same time to whatever music is played. You can introduce free dancing as a challenge about halfway through a semester: "Do you think you could dance to whatever music I put on?" Play some movie background music, some dramatic orchestral music, some rthythmic folk music, and perhaps something classical or popular. Tell the children they must begin to move the minute they hear a sound and when the sound stops they are to hold their shapes and wait for the next selection. No time should be spent thinking or planning; a free dance must be a physical response to the music. Ask them to imagine that the music is coming from inside them and making their bodies move through space. Play a selection for only a few seconds. Then turn the volume off.

Choose selections that differ decidedly in style, texture, and speed. The children find the surprise exciting. Often they bring in their own

These children are "free dancing" to Israeli folk-dance music.

They were asked to change level, direction and shape . . .

and to use any and all body moves and steps.

records. No one watches a free dance, not even the teacher. This dance should be improvisational and purely for personal satisfaction. Your evaluation of each child's development, assimilation of the elements, ability to find variations, make choices, and solve movement problems can be done during the main part of the session as you watch the whole class, half the class, or groups, and as you watch the good-bye dance. Free dancing should remain completely free, by and for the child personally.

When the children have become used to free dancing, perhaps at the end of the semester, ask if they think they can produce enough variety in movement to dance to a record played the whole way through. They will say yes, of course. Impress on them the need for variety. Discuss how they can keep dancing when they are very tired—for instance, by lowering the level to a resting position and moving only one part of the body slowly, using a small amount of space. The one requirement of this dance is that they keep dancing.

The goal is to make dance a part of the children's expression—a complete and fulfilling experience for them. They should dance because it feels good, because they want to move in their own way.

the good-bye dance

For a *good-bye dance* the children line up at the far side of the room and dance to the teacher in any way they wish, as long as they include the element of the day. They must use the space of the room as much as possible and not simply dance in a straight path. They may dance as long as they wish, but must end with a shape. As each one finishes, he or she comes to sit beside the teacher, and the next in line begins.

There always seem to be some children who like to be first and some who like to be last, so lining up does not create trouble. You can start having the children do good-bye dances very early in the term, even on the first day. That first time they may just walk from their places in

"For our good-bye dance today, show me gallops . . .

with *strong* muscles."

line to where you are sitting on the floor; they will make a shape and sit down next to you. Any child can do this, and it means that for a minute you are looking only at that child.

Later you can say, "How else can you walk to me?" Some will come backwards, some will turn, some will walk on two hands and one foot, some on their knees, etc. If at a later date one or two children are embarrassed and do not want to dance, you can let them know that they can just walk if they prefer.

I begin with joyous music for the good-bye dance, and usually, at the start, the children all skip. Folk-dance music and popular music are good here. Later in the term I play any and all kinds of music. The variety is fun, and the children enjoy the challenge.

After they have become secure about dancing and have experimented with many elements, their good-bye dances become spectacular. One day, as they take their seats next to you, they may begin to clap or take up instruments and play along with the music. Some day they may ask to do a good-bye dance for someone who is leaving the school or for someone's birthday. After the last person has danced, if the feeling is really good, then you can say, "Everybody get up and dance together until the music ends." Be prepared for a great surge forward into the space and a climactic group ending!

3

The Priorities

New teachers are usually well prepared with lesson plans. However, the control of behavior problems often is more difficult than carrying out a lesson plan. In order to manage a creative dance class well, the teacher must attract and keep the attention of the children. This is of prime importance because only then can the children become enthusiastic about the subject of dance. When they know you, trust you, and are interested in you, problems in teaching them creative dance decrease.

Most activity periods are between thirty and forty-five minutes long. This means the children must feel secure and enthusiastic about dancing for forty-five minutes! The following "priorities" can help you create such a productive atmosphere. I'll discuss them each in detail in this chapter.

1. *Lay the groundwork.* Show them through movement activities exactly how you will run the class and what you expect from them.

2. *Share the goal.* Tell them what the class is about and what the goal is. We so often forget to let the children in on the plan!

3. *Deal with problems when they occur.* When a child's behavior is not what you want, deal with it immediately; don't wait.

4. *Teach with variety.* Sometimes teach loudly and rapidly, be full of surprises, be quicker than the fastest child. Sometimes teach slowly and softly, with depth. Always use drama! Be ready to watch, to listen, and to challenge. Be ready to change, combine, and supplement lessons.

5. *Evaluate.* Measure the children's progress in relation to the goal. As you make them aware of their achievement, you will be aware of yours.

In all of these, limit your talk, minimize your verbal explanation. Keep the children moving!

LAY THE GROUNDWORK

the "settling in" period

I believe in doing as much preparation as possible before the children enter the room in which they will dance. For example, I have them take off their shoes in the hallway. If this is not feasible, then the taking off of shoes and outer clothing must be considered part of the whole class. There must be a space and a time in which this is done, and some way of beginning class so that the children who are fast at removing their shoes have something to do and a place to be while the slow movers are still getting ready. One teacher fills this time with a drum conversation between herself and the children. Another begins with a blackboard review of the previous lesson. Some teachers have the children jog. Some begin with stories, pictures, or surprises. One teacher I know brings a hat full of lesson ideas and the children draw the lesson for the day from her hat. Any method such as these can use the "settling in" time to advantage.

Playing the drum is a natural invitation for the children to gather around you. Here are two "drum conversations."

activity: echo me

Play something on your drum. Use a phrase of four beats. Ask the children to clap the same sounds with their hands. Start simply, with four even beats. Continue with elementary variations, repeating each one until the children follow perfectly.

slow, slow, slow, slow:	1___ 2___ 3___ 4___
slow, slow, quick, quick, slow:	1___ 2___ 3_ & 4___
slow, slow, very slow:	1___ 2___ 3___
slower, quick, slow, slow:	1___ 2 & 3___ 4

Children don't seem to tire of this activity.

activity: answer me

Use a phrase of eight beats. You play one pattern, the children answer with a different one. (See lesson 24 on learning to make rhythm patterns very simply.) Your phrase and theirs become a rhythmic conversation.

organizing group movement

If it is the children's first class and you are a new teacher, there need to be introductions, conversation, and some finding of common ground, mutual feelings.

In order to lead the class, you must assert power. The colors of your clothes, your voice, or some visual aid can often sustain their attention at the start. If not, find a way to challenge them physically or mentally. As soon as you can, involve their minds and bodies. If something has happened or is happening at the school that claims their attention, talk about it, use it. It may be that what they learn from you through discussion is more important to them and stimulates more learning than would have occurred in your dance class. In other words, children must be with you—attentive to you—before they will become involved in what you ask them to do.

There is a state of being called "a teachable moment." People learn only when they are ready to learn, when the need or the curiosity is there. They won't learn dance if their minds are elsewhere.

Whether you are a classroom teacher or a visiting specialist, it is important to have ground rules that establish the way you and the children will be working together. Any activity that involves large groups of children moving needs organization.

I believe that (1) reaching the children, and (2) establishing a mutually agreed on way of working are so important that they take precedence over your lesson plan. You and the children must experience and agree on the matters set forth in the following sections.

WHERE TO GO AND WHERE NOT TO GO

activity: parade

Play marching music. "Everyone line up behind me and follow the leader!" Proceed to lead them around the walls, behind curtains, through folding chairs, over tumbling mats, under tables. Touch all knobs, open all doors. Duck under the flag, march around the stage. End by skipping over to the record player and sitting on the floor.

When all the children are sitting, ask if there is anything dangerous in the room. Perhaps folding chairs might slide down on them, or there might be metal fixtures protruding from the floor boards. The stage might be dark, dirty, or filled with other people's properties. Decide to stay away from all dangerous places.

Next, establish rules that *you* need. In my classroom I want a private space for my equipment. I want the children to stay away from furniture and to move only where I can see them. Establish *your* minimum ground rules. Having them set up the room for their dance class with you can be an interesting event for children.

HOW TO STOP

activity: run to the wall

"Watch what I can do with my body." Do this yourself or choose a child to do it. Run as fast as you can toward a wall and stop just before you crash into it. "Who thinks he or she can do that?" Choose a child. "Who else?" Choose another. "Dancers can stop their bodies exactly when they want to. Can you? Let's all try that. Line up on this side of the room. When I say go, run as fast as you can and stop just before you hit the wall. Ready, go. Good. No one even had to touch the wall to stop. Now run toward the window [or the railing, the stage, etc.]." Choose directions either to avoid danger or to establish a way of moving together back and forth across the room. Then you can have fun challenging the children: "Are you going to crash into each other? The floor? The ceiling? Of course not; you are dancers, you know how to stop!"

When you have their physical as well as their mental attention, tell them your expectations for the day and for the term. Let them feel your enthusiasm for what is in store for all of you. Let them know the goal of the course and the purpose of all the action to come.

USING SPACE, LISTENING FOR CUES

activity: the eye and ear test

"I think it's time for an eye test. Do you have good eyes? Find an empty space in the room and make a shape. Go. Oh, I still see a large area of empty space. Who sees it too? Who will fill it? Good. Now let's see if you can keep moving among each other, keep walking and always head for the empty spaces. Use your eyes. Turn your head so you can see all around you. Your eyes will lead your body to the empty space. Your eyes are your leaders.

"Now for an ear test. Whenever I play the drum, move just as you were doing. When the drum stops, stop in a shape. Ready, go." Surprise them by playing only a note or two. Continue playing for different lengths of time until all stop when you stop drumming. "If eyes and ears are ready, then many bodies can move together, like a dance company."

activity: near and far
(from Sheila Cogan, Richmond Public Schools, California)

"Come as near to me as you can, without touching, of course. Now go as far from me as you can. Go as near to the record player as you can. As far from the record player. As near to the door. As far." Think of similar directions for your room. "Now here is the test: go as far from all the walls and all the other children as you can. Can you do it? Good. That is how you find your personal space."

CHANGING FORMATIONS

activity: all toes on the black line

Often a class goes well until it is time to change group formation. Transitions are often difficult, for instance the transition from open order formation (all children in their own personal spaces) to a row or rows along the side of the room for locomotor movement in one direction across the floor. It is important to keep the greatest number of children moving. If the room is large enough and the class small enough, conceivably all could skip across the floor simultaneously. Otherwise you could have them go one at a time successively across the floor, with a minimum amount of waiting. The waiting children are the ones who begin to look

The ear test: "When the drum stops, stop in a shape"

for other things to do, so let them call out the counts or clap the beat. Keep them involved!

If the class is large and the space small, you will want to watch a half, a third, or a fourth of the class at a time. Divide them quickly: "Girls in group 1; boys, group 2. Group 1, toes on the black line; group 2 behind them." Or: "All children wearing blue or green, group 1; all wearing red, group 2; all others, group 3. Group 1, toes on black line; group 2 behind them; group 3 behind group 2." Or: "Right half of the room, group 1; left half, group 2," etc.

activity: come to me

Usually, the first time I have the children come to me, they all run and bump into each other. This activity helps. "You learned how dancers can control their bodies, remember? Can you now come to me and sit without touching a single other person? Try it. Run and touch a far wall, and come back to me. Go. Oh, that was much better. Dancers are good at estimating space and time. Now, instead of just coming to me in a bunch, come to me and form a circle sitting on the floor. Can you do that? Ready, run and touch a far wall, then come to me and form a circle. Go."

activity: spread out and face the wall

"Move anywhere you want to in the room. When the drum stops, I'll call, 'Spread out and face the wall!' See if you can do it." Each time you call it out, be in the center of a different wall. They should end in open order formation, using all available space, but all facing the wall, not facing you directly. This puts them in a good position for exercises and all follow-the-leader activities.

Do any or all of the above activities when you need to clarify your system. Invent other activities for your particular children and your special situation.

SHARE THE GOAL

When you have the children's attention, find some interesting way to clarify the goal for the class.

The goals in creative dance are the understanding and use of the elements of dance.

Visual aids can help. You might make a flower of construction paper with each petal being a different element to be explored during the term. The stem could be "energy," for energy must go up through that stem to feed the blossom of a plant. Just so, energy is needed in dance. In addition to the element petals, a leaf or two could be "variety," for without variety dance would be boring.

Another visual aid might be a rocket ship exploring space, with each star a different element of dance. Another could be a box containing surprise packages. Hide the names of the elements under the petals, stars or packages until the specific lesson on that element is taught. In this way, the children can see their progress and can see how much they have yet to learn.

Dance is not only a physical activity. It also involves the mind and the spirit. When there is more than one dancer, it becomes a social activity.

Much more learning takes place in a dance class than just the knowledge and use of the elements. I find it is a good time to teach concentration, self-discipline, and responsibility. These become additional goals. It is imperative that the children learn these things for their own personal growth and in order to receive optimum benefit from the classes.

I find students need to relate these ideas, like the rules for group movement, to very direct experiences. I teach and refer to concentration, self-discipline, and responsibility often and in very simple ways, as in the following examples.

concentration

activity: if a rhinoceros comes . . .

Some dance rooms have open doors and windows. Some seem to be actual corridors while class is going on. If interruptions occur and cause the children to turn their focus away from you or the project at hand, take the time to explain about concentration. What does that word mean?

Teach them that dancers use their minds when they use their bodies. They concentrate. "So, class, do we pay attention if someone knocks on the door? No! We are dancers and we are concentrating on dance. Even if a rhinoceros comes, do we look up? No! We are dancers. Will you help each other remember that?"

self-discipline

activity: no gum

"Why don't dancers chew gum while dancing? They could swallow it or choke if they are jumping. It might fall out and be stepped on, with bare feet!" You might elicit even more answers from the children. "Can you remember to throw away gum before you come into the dance room? When you do it by yourself, that is self-discipline. That is helping yourself to become a better person and a better dancer. Tell me if you do remember that by yourself. I'd like to know. In the beginning, we'll all help each other to remember."

Sometimes children push and shove or squeeze in front of someone in line, invading another's "personal space." Stress the use of self-discipline here: "Dancers use self-discipline to control their bodies and their actions."

Children can learn to be neat about placing their shoes and outer clothing so that these are not in the way; they can learn not to interrupt a class and not to pull away from the group activity; they can learn to control the urge to laugh at others; they can learn not to fall and slide haphazardly; they can learn to dance "full out," to stretch higher and to balance longer. Stressing self-discipline in movement helps a growing child.

At the end of a session you might have them think for a moment if they used self-discipline in any way, and you might comment on actions (not people) that you noticed.

activity: partner support

Partner A agrees to support B as he or she tries balancing in different positions. "See how far off balance you can go while your partner holds you. How far into space can you reach? What can you do when someone is helping you that you can't do all by yourself? Partner A has the responsibility to keep B from falling. Show B that you are responsible, you are trustworthy, you are dependable." Partners then change places, and B supports A.

"What does responsibility mean? Your parents are bringing you up. You are responsible or answerable to them. You have life and talent; you are responsible or accountable to the best part of yourself. You are a member of this class; you are responsible to the group. The group needs your support just like your partner did in the exercise.

"Dancers support each other and help each other. What are some ways we can do that?"

Add these concepts, or others that you feel are important, to your visual aid. It helps to have goals clearly in sight.

DEAL WITH PROBLEMS

Once ground rules have been established, it is of utmost importance to keep reestablishing them. The class must always meet your minimum requirements for behavior.

I had one little girl who would go up on the stage because she knew we had a rule not to go on the stage. I stopped the class, and we reestablished the rule, with the reasons. The next day she did it again. The following day I told her I would help her not to go on the stage, and I held her hand often during the class. The whole class spent quite a bit of time talking about rules, groups, and working together as a family or as a dance company. If we hadn't done that, I think this child would have found more significant ways to be different and disruptive. As it was, she knew that she was noticed, different, and that we wanted her in the group.

Once a child climbed the basketball fixture. There is no way to conduct a class when this happens! It is then time to stop teaching dance and to teach something else—awareness of each other, self-discipline, acceptable ways to show feelings, anger, energy.

There was one child who continually pushed to be in front of any line and continually invaded others' personal space. Again, this action is speaking so loudly for attention that it is far more important—for the individual child and the rest of the children—for the teacher to deal with this problem than to try to teach dance. It is a "teachable moment" for all in the class.

I have learned that a child's wants are very close to his or her needs. Some children have needs that are greater than or far different from those of the rest of the group. Those are the children you must deal with. They are also the children the group must deal with. I have found that classes understand this, and, once it is revealed that some children really do need to be first in line more than the others, the rest can accept it. When we talked about it in my particular class, we decided that Sue could be first whenever she needed to be first. Then another child spoke up and informed us that she too needed to be first! So they divided the time. After that, I saw to it that I did activities in ways other than one at a time.

I had one child who always ran out of the room during class. When I talked to her I discovered that my drum gave her a headache. I learned to play different instruments and to play them more softly.

I suggest that you try hard to establish comfortable ways of working and to reach all the children all the time. It does not work if any child separates from the group. All must dance, unless something is really wrong, and, if so, you must handle that problem. First you must deal with whatever is in the way of group dancing. The children must be a group who will dance under your leadership. Anything less is futile and therefore unacceptable.

TEACH WITH VARIETY

Now that you have laid the groundwork, have shared the goal, and are dealing immediately with problems, it is time to look at the lessons and the way you teach.

If class periods are forty-five minutes, you will need more than the lessons written here. Precede them with some stimulating activity, such as jogging or skipping. Follow that with full body stretching. This general warm-up serves to pull the group together, and also provides a ritual opening to center the children's minds and bodies and to begin their concentration on dance.

Toward the end of class, after the children have worked creatively on the element for the day, be sure to have them spend some time as audience, watching each other's work. Follow that period by one of large free locomotor movements across the floor, such as runs, leaps, and skips. End the class with a free dance or a good-bye dance and a "cool-down"—stretching once more, with some attention to rhythmic breathing.

In effect, then, a class plan would look like this:

10 minutes   Stimulating warm-up: free whole body moves, such as running, swinging, shaking, skipping, followed by stretching

20 minutes   Element for the day: presentation, exploration, use in form, audience review

10 minutes   Steps across the floor, free dance, good-bye dance

5 minutes   Cool-down: stretching, breathing

Use this general outline, or make your own lesson plan, using your particular knowledge and skills.

Don't let yourself be bored by the children, and don't let them be bored by you. I am bored if I don't see variety in their dancing. Perhaps they are bored if they don't see variety in me!

Bring in visual aids, use different instruments to accompany them, use new records, but most of all try to really *see* the children's movement. It sometimes happens that we teach without actually seeing what is going on. We teach as if driven by some machine, going through a lesson for the sake of the lesson. Whom do you look at when you teach? How much do you see?

Most teachers watch students who move with skill, conviction, or variety. Can you help others to move like that? What exactly are the weaker students doing?

If we try to teach the children in front of us and are not satisfied until they improve in skill, conviction, or variety, then we are really teaching and will be driven by the students rather than by a lesson plan. This means that we are forced to use ingenuity to find the right words, the right images, the right inspiration to reach particular children. When we do this, variety and enthusiasm are by-products, and good teaching results.

So, first see what is happening in front of you. Improve it any way you can. Don't be satisfied with less than exciting dancing.

I find that I make arbitrary rules in order to achieve excitement in movement. For instance, I often announce, "No running." I am bored by plain running. Sometimes the children bore me by continually skipping. If a class seems lethargic, add the element of speed. If they are moving with constant energy, add stops. Whatever the movement needs for variety, add it. Subtract what is boring.

This means you will jump from lesson to lesson. What difference does that make, as long as you are progressing on the road to dynamic dancing? If the children are looking at each other and giggling, teach focus. Do whatever you need to do to make good dance happen right then before your eyes.

Teach the children to see as you see, and let them help you to see. Can they express verbally what they see? Can they express what they feel when dancing or when watching movement? Can you? Talk with the children in class. At this point you are not "teaching" them or "telling" them something. You are sharing a conversation. This is not only educational, it is a welcome change!

So let variety come two ways: by your preparation and thought, and by seeing and dealing with the movement happening in front of you.

EVALUATE

Evaluate means to examine or judge, to assess by critical judgment. In dance, the eyes are the tool for evaluation. You will need to watch the children closely to see if they know the difference between a skip and a gallop (lesson 4), to see if their walk is exactly with the drum beat (lesson 7), to see if they are collapsing or bending (lesson 12). You will need to know the children's movement habits in order to judge whether or not they are challenging their bodies and moving with variety. All during class your eyes will be assessing what is happening.

Then at the end of class, you can "test" them during the good-bye dance. If the lesson has been on straight and curved pathways (lesson 20), ask them to put curves into their good-bye dance. Then watch to see that their bodies lean into the curve, that they can do large sweeping curves, and small tight curves, and that they can change the direction of the curve by the lean of the body.

Watch first to see if their bodies are doing the movement you ask for. Then watch to see that their minds are making them do the movement with variety in level, direction, speed, and force. Finally, watch their facial expressions to see if they are dancing with feeling, with spirit, with emotion.

First, accomplish the physical motion with clarity. Your teaching is then adequate. Next, involve their minds with the movement. Your teaching is then challenging. Finally, involve their spirit. Your teaching is then inspirational!

The accomplishments become progressively harder, because the lessons are cumulative. That is, in lesson 1, having the children make a variety of energetic shapes is sufficient. However, the children must continue to vary their shapes when they come to show rising and collapsing (lesson 12). A knowledge of rising and collapsing movements without varying shapes would be incomplete and therefore unsatisfactory.

As you watch their work at the end of each lesson, check whether the children include all the elements previously learned. This means you must train your eyes and your memory as they train their minds and their muscles!

Besides being able to show the element physically, children should be able to describe it and to relate it to other things. They should connect elements of dance to the world around them by noticing that clouds are moving shapes, cars stop and go, balloons rise and collapse.

In a lesson, then, there are four times when you can evaluate the students' understanding of an element: first, during the exploratory section; second, during the "form" section, when they perform their shape—movement—shape dance; third, when they describe "what moves like that"; and fourth, during the good-bye dance.

The understanding and use of the elements of dance are the first goals of creative dance. In addition, we have set the goals of concentration, self-discipline, and responsibility. The child's growth in these areas can also be evaluated. How long can Jessie concentrate on dance? Did she giggle less today and put more strength into her moves? Is Mike falling and sliding less often? Is he disciplining his body better? Is Joe cooperating in the class project? Does he feel group responsibility?

Children often like to see their progress in writing. A chart on the wall listing their names vertically and the goals and elements horizontally can help. One teacher I know has such a chart, and the children show her their efforts whenever they are ready. When they do well, she draws a star under that goal or element with five lines. When they do not do well, she draws a part of a star using perhaps three lines. If they even try, she draws at least one line. They can always go back and complete the stars.

An obvious benefit of evaluating the children's progress is that we teachers assess not only our ability to communicate but also our ability to see. The art of seeing is an important adjunct to the art of teaching. So often we see what we want to see or what we expect to see. I remember a teacher who used to say, "Stand straight and tall"; then, although half the class was not standing "straight and tall," she went on with her lesson.

We must be able to communicate—to explain verbally what we want from the children—but we must also be able to evaluate—to see and to judge what they have accomplished and how far they have come in relation to the goal.

4

The Lessons

LESSONS BASED ON ELEMENTS

The lessons described here are "nuggets": short and directed to one goal. They were done with groups of twenty to thirty children in periods of approximately thirty minutes.

Shapes are done first because they become the beginning and end of every movement, they are a basic part of all subsequent lessons, and they are basic control. "Stop and go" is done next because it establishes how to move freely around the room without disturbing others. After these two basic lessons, you can proceed in any order that seems to work.

Every teacher is different, just as every child is different. Please use these nuggets as takeoff points for your own variations. Use them only as much as they help. Above all, teach each lesson in your own way, just as you wish each child to dance in her or his own way. (Let me know how you do; I'd like to hear from you. Write to Mary Joyce, c/o Mayfield Publishing Company, 285 Hamilton Avenue, Palo Alto, CA 94301.)

To plan your lesson, first choose an element, then find a helper. The elements are constant; the helpers you select to teach them will vary.

choosing an element

Decide what element to teach by considering (1) what the children will respond to, (2) the needs of their age group, (3) the needs of some individuals in the group, (4) the general movement ability of the children, or (5) what follows naturally from the previous lesson.

Do not be afraid of repetition. Each lesson must build upon the previous one. Although the elements repeat themselves over and over again, the way in which the children use the elements will change. Children love repetition. One week we did "living sculptures" based on use of muscles. The following week I had planned to go on to breath movement, but the children insisted on repeating living sculptures.

This very often happens with beginning groups. They get a sense of security and of accomplishment from repetition. So do not be afraid to work on any lesson until it is well assimilated. It is also a good idea to drop a lesson and skip to the next if the class does not respond well. Enthusiastic class response is the prime object. The way in which you reach this goal will change with every group.

finding a helper

When you have decided on the element for the lesson, next find a *helper*. A helper is an image or a way of working. It makes an element more interesting and more fun. It can clarify a dance movement or be a vehicle through which an element is used. A lesson without a helper runs the risk of being uninteresting, unclear, or static.

Names are used to help children recall learning. Think of a helper as "packaging the learning." *Living sculpture* is a helper for use of muscles. The words *mirrors* and *twins* can help the class see two different ways of working in twos.

Names also help the teacher. The names *graveyard, spaghetti monster,* and *writing in space* can help you remember where you are heading in your lesson plan.

You know the *goal* and how to *structure*. Now, prepared with an *element* and a *helper,* you are ready to teach creative dance.

LESSONS BASED ON ELEMENTS

"Now let me see a one-legged shape." Although most of the
children are finding their balance by leaning forward, the girl
in the center tries leaning backward.

74 *the lessons*

element: shapes

helper: crossovers

As you sit here on the floor around me, notice that your body is making a shape in space. The shape you are sitting in is different from the next person's. I'm going to count to three. On three, I want you to sit in a different shape. One, two, three. Good. Find another shape. One, two, three.

This time, find an unusual shape, maybe standing, or lying, or squatting. Ready, one, two, three. Oh my! There are some bent shapes, some stretched shapes, some twisted shapes! Let's do that again. One, two, three. Oh, some more strange shapes.

Now put muscles into those shapes, so you can feel them. You can hold that shape even if a large bird should land on you. If I put some weight on you, you could hold it up. Show me as I come around.

There's one at a low level. Let's all make a shape at a low level. Ready, get set, go. Hold very still, so I can see those shapes. Put some air under your shape and through your shape. Can you lift your center off the floor? Can you feel how that makes your muscles work?

Now let me see a high level shape, as high as you can go in space and hold still. Think about muscles and air spaces through your shape.

Now show me a shape you've never been in before in your whole life. Go. Oh no, wait a minute. I'm sure you've been in that shape before. Come on, show me a really strange shape, one you thought you could never do. Go. Oh, much better.

Now let me see a one-legged shape. An upside-down shape. A stretched shape—everything must stretch, your fingers, your ankles. Now a bent shape. How many different bent shapes can you make with your arms? Your legs? Your whole body? Make a twisted shape. Can you make a round shape?

Do you suppose you could move around among each other and not touch a single person? Dancers and athletes can move slowly or quickly in a crowd without any bumping. Let's try it. Walk slowly. When the drum stops, you stop and make a shape. Ready, go. *(Repeat with gallops or skips.)*

This time let me see you change levels as you move through space, sometimes low, sometimes high. Go. Now try making shapes with your whole body as you walk. Go anywhere you want to go, in and out among each other, never touching a single person. You can twist and turn, walk forward or sideward or backward. When the drum stops, hold a shape.

Now that you know some movements, let's put them together and make a dance of shapes. We'll use still shapes and moving shapes. First, everyone show me your most interesting starting shape. Go. Good. Some are low, some are high. Now moving shapes. Go. You're moving through space, changing levels, changing directions, changing shapes, using all the parts of your body, twisting, stretching, bending. When the drum stops, make an ending shape.

Now let's divide the class in half and watch each other. Let's watch the interesting shapes and see how many different ways each of us can move.

Goals for evaluation: Stress that the children use their muscles consciously, because that is the way people feel and remember movement. Look for still shapes that are a physical challenge to the child's own body. Look for full use of backbone in moving shapes.

elements: directions, tempo

helper: stop and go

Look around the room and see the open space. See the space that is empty. When I say go, move out, find some empty space and make a shape. Fill some space with your shape. Ready, go.

John, while everyone is holding a shape, can you move in and out, around and between those shapes? Can you still find the empty space in the room? Can you move through it? Go. Jill and Bev, join John. Find the empty space. Find where your body can fit. Change your moving shape to fit the space. *(Keep adding more and more children. Soon all are moving, there are no more still shapes.)*

Do you always have to move forward? In what other directions can you move? Let me see you move sideward. Backward. Better watch behind you. Let me see you make some turns. And make a shape.

Show me how slowly a human being can move. How fast? Now slow motion again. Can you change your tempo, your speed, without me telling you when? Go. Remember, athletes and dancers have good control of their bodies and can change direction and speed as they move. Keep it smooth, between and around the other moving shapes. Can you change direction when you change your speed? Try it.

What else can you do besides walk? Can you hop? How slowly can you hop? Can you skip? Can you skip backward? Sideward? Jump! Show me a jump turn. Now show me how many ways you can change your movements before the drum stops—that's variety. Show me variety. Ready, go.

Now when I call your name, stop and make a shape. Everyone else keep moving, keep filling the empty space. *(Call names until all are still.)*

"Stay inside the circle, move among each other, and find the open space. How many can fit inside the circle and keep moving with variety? Forward, sideward, backward, turning. Slow sometimes, then fast."

The stops are as interesting as the moves! Let's make a stop-and-go dance. Instead of just stopping at the end of your movements, put some stops in between your moves. Stops must be interesting shapes. Make them so interesting that I want to stop and look at them. Make me see your stops. Hold a few seconds, then move again. Do you have to stop when someone else does? No. You stop whenever you want to. We'll always have some people stopped and others moving. Ready, begin.

You have been using the whole room. Let's see what happens if we use a small space. Let me see you five do "stop and go" inside this circle on the floor. Go. And make a shape. Good. I saw fast turns and good dodges. I saw variety in direction and speed and some exciting stops. Do you think you can do it now without making it look like a dodging game? Show me how easy you can make it look. Keep it smooth, no jerks. Let's add five more people. *(Keep adding children until the whole class is inside the circle.)* And make an ending shape.

Good. That showed control of moving and stopping, and there was lots of variety in direction and tempo.

Goals for evaluation: Look for variety and self-challenge.

"Hurry back to your spot—thirteen, fourteen, fifteen."

element: place

helper: fifteen counts

Each person stand on one spot in the room—any spot. Now look where you are and memorize that spot. Look for marks on the floor. Look where you are in relation to the door, the windows, the posts. Now I'm going to give you fifteen counts. I'll beat fifteen times on my drum, and I'll count out loud. You may go anywhere at all in the room, but you must be on your very same spot on count fifteen. Ready, go. One, two *(count through),* fifteen.

Say, that wasn't so easy, was it? Shall we try that again? This time I'll only give you twelve counts. How many? Twelve. Go. One *(count through),* twelve.

Much better. Now let's see how much you can do in those twelve counts. How much space can you cover? How much air in this room can you touch and still be back by twelve? Let's see. One *(count through),* twelve.

Wonderful. I saw people reaching and bending and changing directions and touching all parts of the space in this room, and no one touched anyone else. Let me see what you can do in twenty counts. This time, I want to see you move in interesting shapes, moving sometimes on the floor, sometimes at walking level, and sometimes in the air. Show me what you can do. This time let's start in a shape and end in a shape. Ready, one *(count through),* twenty.

Let's divide in half now and watch each other. Fifteen counts this time. Let's see how different people gauge how much space they can use in fifteen counts. *(Count.)*

Now I want to see how much you can do in fifteen counts without moving off your spot! Think of all the parts of the body you can move, think of changing levels, think of bending, stretching, twisting, turning, sometimes moving fast, sometimes very, very slowly. Ready, go. *(Count.)*

Take a partner. Stand on spots right next to each other. Decide who is number 1 and who is number 2. The first time I play fifteen counts, number 1 will move through space, while number 2 moves on the spot. End with a shape. Then number 2 will dance through space, and number 1 will move on the spot. Let's try it. Ready, go. *(Count.)* Now change. *(Count.)*

Let's divide in half again, and this time we'll watch the duets.

Goals for evaluation: Look for variety of moves and the ability to estimate time and space.

element: steps

helper: shapes

Go anywhere you want to go in the room. When the drum stops, make a shape. Head for the open spaces—fill the whole room! Ready, go. And make a shape.

This time you have to walk, but show me walking in many directions, with body shapes. Go. Shape.

In order to make good shapes while doing steps, that spine has to move. Show me how you can move your back. Arch it. Round it. Twist it. Lean to the side. This time, I want you to run, not only changing directions, but also trying to make shapes with your back. Go. And shape.

What is leaping? Yes, a high, wide run. Let's take several runs and a leap. Go. Let's do it again. Can you make a shape when you're in the air? Can you leap sideward? Backward?

Jumping: remember, jumping is landing with two feet at the same time. Make shapes as you jump. How many ways can you jump? With crossed feet? With feet together? Feet apart? Small jumps? Big jumps? Let's see what can happen with jumping. Go. Shape.

Show me hopping. Can you hop and turn? Can you hop slowly? Can you hop and make shapes? How many ways can you move your arms as you hop? Ready, go. Shape.

Skipping: what can you do with a skip? *(Etc.)*

Galloping: how many ways can you gallop? *(Etc.)*

Sliding: slide out that foot as you start. What can you do with a slide? *(Etc.)*

Everyone line up on the black line ready to come all at once across

"Come across the floor two at a time, jumping and making shapes."

"All at once. Come across the floor and combine at least two steps.
Change level, direction, or tempo." The boy at the right is doing a forward
run, while the boy on the left is jumping sideward.

"What shape will you make as you leap over the drumstick?"

the room. Combine at least two steps before you reach the far side of the room. What are the steps? Walk, run, leap, jump, hop, skip, gallop, slide. Make your steps interesting by changing your level or your direction or your tempo. Always make shapes. Ready. See what you can do.

Now come two at a time so you can watch each other. Ready, first two.

Today let's do a good-bye dance. Do any steps you like, and come one at a time from your side of the room over to where I am sitting on the floor. Make a shape when you reach me, and then sit next to me. As soon as the person ahead of you finishes, you can start. Ready. *(Play some lively music.)* Go.

Goals for evaluation: Look for clarity of footwork.

"Rise, slow motion, with
every muscle tight."

element: muscles

helper: living sculpture

Everyone sit in exactly the same shape as I am. *(Sit on the floor hugging your knees.)* Now, no matter what I say or what you do, the one thing you must not do is change your shape.

I am going to count to seven. While I count, you are going to make your muscles tighter and tighter. By the time I get to seven, you will feel that every muscle is as tight as possible. You will feel your stomach, your back, your shoulders, your cheeks, your fingers, your thighs, your toes—everything. Are you ready? Can you change your shape while you do this? No! After I count to seven, then I'll count back down to one, and you'll gradually get looser and limper. Ready? Sit now in the shape as limply as you can, just barely hold on, and here we go, getting tighter and tighter. One *(count through)*, seven. Seven *(count through)*, one.

Tell me: what parts of your body did you feel? Now let's do it once more and try to feel all of your body, not just some parts. Be sure to tighten your stomach and your thighs. Those two places are most important. Ready, shape. One *(count through)*, seven. Seven *(count through)*, one. Did you feel your stomach and thighs?

Now we are going to use these muscles to make us do things we never thought possible. Get into a shape from which you can rise easily. I'll play some muscle music *(percussive or electronic music is good for this study)*, and you rise, slow motion, with every muscle tight. Remember, especially your thigh and stomach muscles. As you rise, you can twist and bend and stretch and try holding your balance on one leg. Try holding your balance in fantastic shapes. You'll be able to do it because you are using your muscles. If you lose your balance, catch yourself with your muscles and start again. Never get limp or loose.

These children are making slow-motion twisting moves
as they change levels in "living sculpture."

Ready? We'll rise and come down, that's all—no going through space. Tighten those muscles and make all the shapes you can as you rise in slow motion. When the music stops, hold your shape.

(Play music. While the children dance, comment.) Slower. Now slower. Make that body hold on to the shapes. Try something harder: try standing on one leg, and see how many slow-motion shapes you can find. How can you go back down, still using muscles? Go down some different way, using your thighs to control your slow movement. *(Stop the music.)* What did that feel like? Were you aware of your muscles? Which ones?

Now we are going to do the same thing—rise once and descend once—but you are going to be living sculpture. Do you know what a sculpture is? I am going to unveil all these new works of art, and we shall watch the latest masterpieces of living sculpture. Take a low shape now, and imagine yourself covered with a black velvet cloth. As the music starts, imagine I am unveiling you for the first time, and begin to move slowly with muscles up through space. When you have moved to high level, then slowly return to low level. Do as many movements as you can between high and low. Then hold your low shape until everyone finishes. I'll wait for everyone, so don't hurry. Ready. *(Start the music. When music stops, comment.)* Oh, I saw some good slow-motion shapes, some beautiful twisting ones, and strong use of thigh muscles.

Let's watch each other. This half of the class first. Now the other half. Remember to concentrate on what you are dancing. Your mind and your body are concentrating on just one thing. *(Music and comments.)*

For a good-bye dance today, let's move our muscles through space. Let's do monster muscles: you must be the most frightening monster I have ever seen, and I must see some jumps and some low level shapes. *(Play music or the drum.)*

Goals for evaluation: Look for attempts to make new moves and find balances that are different.

"Rise as you breathe in, then exhale and drop." The girl has found the suspended feeling of breath movement, while the boy in the background is dropping.

lesson **6**

element: breath

helper: ideas from children

Besides your muscles, there is something else in your body that deter-mines how you move. Does anyone have any idea what that might be? *(Go into the lesson that corresponds to whatever they say first: heart, bones and joints, or breath.)*

When you breathe, you move. Everyone take a big breath. Which way did your body move? *(Usually the children say "Up and down" or "In and out.")* Now try to get that breath movement into your *arm.* Imagine inflating your arm with air. Let it rise. And fall. Do that with your head. Let it rise. Then fall. Your chest. Your leg.

Now you can take a very long breath, or a short, panting breath. Get on one spot, and put yourself into a position from which you can rise. Take one long breath, hold it, then let it out. Let your body follow by rising, suspending the movement, then falling. Ready, go. Do it again in a different shape, maybe add a turn or a balance on one leg. Now try letting your breath take you only halfway up.

Now that you have the feeling, you don't have to keep breathing in time with the movement. Your throat will get rather dry and you'll tire quickly. Try rising and falling, now, up to different levels, using the feeling of inflating your body or parts of your body with air. Let them collapse—really collapse. Then start again. Try some short gasps, and some long, long breaths. I won't play the drum or play any record this time so that you can feel the rhythm and timing of the rise and fall of your breath. Each of you will be different. Remember to keep your eyes on your own body, or on the air around you. Try not to look directly at someone else. We'll watch each other later. Ready, shape, begin.

The feeling of the breath impulse in movement is sometimes hard to find. This boy is holding his breath and his shape by muscle tension. Instead, he should exhale and let the downward movement follow naturally.

What do you know that moves like that? *(Answers have been: a kite, a cloud, a butterfly, the ocean, a paper airplane.)* Everyone take one of these ideas or any other that you think of and dance it by using the breath impulse and letting go. Ready, shape, begin.

What is the difference between being yourself dancing on your own breath, and being something else, like a cloud or a kite? How is the feeling different? This time you can be either yourself or something you imagine. Concentrate as deeply as you can on what you are trying to do, on the kind of movement that we are doing. Show me lots of changes this time—changes in level and in your use of space around the room. Change your tempo. too. Try leaping, skipping, or jumping on the breath impulse. Try running. Show me variety in your movements this time. Ready, go.

Now let's watch each other, because there are so many different and beautiful movements and shapes. Watch and see if you can get the feeling of breath impulse from the dancers. First half, ready, shape, begin. *(Comment.)* Second half, ready, shape, begin. *(The dancing may take place either unaccompanied or with music.)*

Goals for evaluation: Look for lightness and free flow in rising and falling. There should be good use of knee bends in all landings.

"Imagine the floor is your drum and the sounds you are making are very even. March anywhere you want to in the room and feel the steadiness of the beat."

element: beat

helper: heart

What else in your body is moving all the time? Your heart. Everyone, jump. Jump a few times and make your heartbeat strong. Whose heart can I feel? Jane? *(Beat the tempo of Jane's heart on the drum.)* Everyone, clap to Jane's heartbeat. Everyone, jump again. Whose heart can I feel? Albert? Everyone march to Albert's heartbeat.

Now feel your own heartbeat. Let's be very quiet so each of us can feel our own heartbeats. When you feel yours, tap your knee with your finger in time to it. You may have to close your eyes to feel it and not be distracted by something else.

Now, your heartbeat is a very even beat. What does "even" mean? Can you make your head move evenly in time with your heart? Move your arms evenly in time. Your feet. Let's all clap evenly. Now let's march—marching is moving your feet with an even beat. Imagine the floor is your drum and the sounds you are making are very even. March anywhere you want to in the room and feel the steadiness of the beat. Feel how each foot stays the same length of time on the floor. The lengths of time are even. Ready, go.

Now march with your head. Your arms. Your elbows. Knees. Hips. Back. Fingers. Move in time to this music. *(Play a march.)*

Who can move just that evenly, but twice as slowly? Try it. Move on every other beat, staying with the music. Now try it without the music. Slow, even beat. You can move through space or up and down in levels. Keep making interesting shapes as you move slowly but evenly.

Now move with your heartbeat again, the medium beat.

Who can move exactly twice as fast? Go. With your feet. Now with your arms. Head. Hands.

Now with the march music we are going to have variety. *(Play music.)* Let's all be medium, first. Go. Show me how many different kinds of even movement you can do at a medium speed. Now move to the slow beat—exactly twice as slow as medium. Now twice as fast. *(Stop the music.)*

What can you think of that moves evenly like that? What is there besides your heart that keeps a steady even beat? *(Answers have been: robots, drops of water, machines.)* Take one of these ideas and dance it. Remember: concentration and variety. Go.

Now take a partner. One of you will do breath movement, and one will do heartbeat movement. Decide who will do which. Show me your starting shape. Ready, go. And make an ending shape.

Practice again. Make sure you have a definite ending shape. Know how you are going to end. Don't be afraid to whisper to each other if you have to. Ready, shape, begin. Everyone show me your ending shape. Good, I think we are ready. Let's watch these duets. Watchers, see if you can tell who is doing heartbeat and who is doing breath.

Goals for evaluation: Watch for children who may be having a hard time matching their movements to the music. In the partner dances, look for differentiation between breath and beat.

element: bones and joints

helper: graveyard

Today I want you to imagine you have no muscles at all. You are just a bag of bones. Show me a shape those bones can make. Another shape. Yes, those bones would dangle and hang loosely. Each bone is hanging from its own joint.

Let's start from your center—that's your backbone or spine. How many ways can those spine bones move? They can arch, they can bend, they can twist or turn, they can curve sidewards. Can they circle? Can they do two things at once? Try it.

Now go to your shoulder joint. What comes out of the shoulder joint? What can your arms do? The hip joint—what can your legs do? Is there anything your arms can do that your legs can't? Let's go farther from your center, to your elbows and knees. Can they do all the things your shoulders and hips can do? Let's go farther still, to your ankles and wrists, then to your fingers and toes. What can they do? Your head—it's right at the top of your backbone. What does your neck joint let your head do?

Now go anywhere in the room and show me how many ways your joints let your bones move. They can bend, they can reach, they can lift, they can fall, they can twist, they can shake, they can swing, they can circle. Let me see you gallop with free, shaking bones. Skip. Hop. Jump. Leap. Yes, keep them loose and free. You have no muscles to make the movement strong or tight.

Back to your spot, now, and let me see you move just your arms as if they were nothing but sticks tied to their joints by string. Now move the joints and bones of your spine. Now your neck. Your legs, arms.

Your feet, fingers. Let me see one high jump, and while you are in the air, shake every bone in your body. Ready, go.

Your bones give your body its shape in space. There is no energy in bones as there is in muscles. Let me see you move your bones slowly now into different shapes. Hold your shape just a floppy second, and then fall into another shape. Use as little effort as you can. Feel as if you are moving the skeleton of your body. Go.

Imagine that you are all skeletons in the graveyard. At midnight you rise and dance a most fantastic dance of bones. When you end, show me how you get back into your coffin. Remember: just bones and joints, no muscles. Think of loose shapes in space. Ready, go. *(For music use novelty percussion or rhythm sticks or beat the rim of your drum.)*

What do you know besides yourself that moves loosely in shapes like bones? *(Answers have been: puppets, scissors, lightning.)* Let's take partners now, and do another duet. This half of the class will watch first. This time both partners may be bones, or one may be muscles. Surprise us, and let's see if the watchers can tell what kind of movement you are doing. Make it very clear whether you are using your muscles or your bones. Practice about two minutes. *(Performance and comments.)*

For our good-bye dance today, come to me without using your feet! Discover how muscles and bones and joints all work together.

Goals for evaluation: Look for looseness and freedom.

element: levels

helper: rhythmic words

When I tell you to go, I want you to drop to the floor and hold your shape. Ready, get set, go. Let's do that again and find a different low shape. Ready, get set, go.

This time I want you to melt down to the floor, slowly and smoothly. Go.

Now let's put a jump before the fall. It will be: jump, fall. You can drop or you can melt, slowly or quickly. Ready, jump, fall. Oh, let's see more interesting jumping shapes. Give me two jumps, each one different—making a different shape or facing a different direction. Ready, go. Now the words will be: jump, jump, fall, shape. Ready, jump, jump, fall, shape.

Take a resting shape on the floor, and, when I say go, be standing. No, don't prepare—really see what your body has to do to muster enough strength to get up fast. Remember, don't start before I say go, and don't move after I say go—make it that fast! See how far you can get in one count. Ready, go. Good.

Start in a low shape again, and this time, melt up from low level to standing, slowly and smoothly. Ready, go. Let's put in a roll on the floor before you get up. Ready, roll, and up.

Now the words will be: jump, jump, fall, shape, roll, and come up. The roll will give you some momentum so you'll come up easily. Let's try that part. Take a shape on the floor. Give yourself a push, roll over, and come up. Another way to get momentum is to swing your legs back over your head and come up to your knees. Try it. Lie down on your back. Go.

"Melt down to the floor, slowly and smoothly." Each of the
children found a different way to reach floor level. Then each
holds the shape, waiting until all have finished.

Here we go with the sequence. Ready, jump, jump, fall, shape, roll, and come up. There are eight words, and I'll say them evenly. Make your movement fit the words.

Now let's add: walk, walk, walk, walk, t-u-r-n, and shape. I'll make that fit eight counts too.

Line up on the black line and come across the floor with the whole sequence: jump, jump, fall, shape, roll, and come up; walk, walk, walk, walk, t-u-r-n, and shape. Make your movement fit the rhythm of the words. Everyone say the words with me: jump, jump, fall, shape, roll, and come up; walk, walk, walk, walk, t-u-r-n, and shape.

Now do the moves and say the words. Feel what your body has to do to change levels that quickly. Ready, go. *(Say the words.)*

We've talked about low level—body on the floor—and high level—body standing or in the air. Middle level is kneeling or squatting. Show me a middle level shape. Go. This time, make your own sequence, and add some middle level movements. A sequence is a sentence of movements. Take a minute and practice. Put some levels and some steps together so you can move across the room. You won't have to say the words, just do the moves. See if you can make a sentence and repeat it. Practice.

Now come two at a time across the floor. This will be our good-bye dance—a dance of levels.

Goals for evaluation: Watch for skill in transition from one movement to the next. Also look for good use of momentum and flow.

"Leaders, move slowly and clearly so your mirrors can
follow you." Most children are still working with arms and hands
and have not changed level. The two boys who can barely
be seen in center have found a change of direction.

element: body parts

helper: mirrors

Everyone spread out in the room. Let me see you shake your whole body. Go. Stop. Now let me see a stretch with your whole body. Now a bend. A twist. A collapse. A swing. A sway. A shake again.

Today we are going to isolate parts of our body. That means we are going to move one part separately, all by itself. Let's try the head first. In order to move your head, what else has to move? Where are the muscles that move your head? In your neck. So let's isolate head and neck. Show me how many ways you can move your head. I'll say "head" but you'll know I mean "head and neck." Can you stretch it? How many ways can you bend it? Can you turn it? Roll it? Twist it? Can you shake it slowly? Fast? How big a movement can you do with your head? How small?

Now your shoulders: lift them. Lift them one at a time. Roll them. Push them back. Push them down. What else can you do with your shoulders? How fast can they move? How slowly?

Your arms: show me all the ways you can think of to move them. Stretch. Bend them. Twist them. Move them through space. Swing them. Sway them. Shake them. Lift them. Let them collapse. Circle them.

Your back: how many ways can you move that backbone? That will put you into all kinds of interesting shapes, won't it? Try moving your back and your shoulders together. Now your back and your shoulders and arms. Now your back and shoulders and arms and head.

Your hands: do a hand dance in front of your face. How many shapes can you make with your hands? Can they dance through space? Behind you? On the floor?

What about your legs? How many ways can they move? Lie down on your back and see what they can do. Stand on one leg and see what the other can do. Let me see it stretch. Now bend. Now the other leg.

Now let me see slow-motion legs. When you think you might lose your balance, carefully and slowly change to the other leg. Keep moving that free leg through the space, twisting, stretching, bending, swinging, swaying, and shaking. Try everything. Go. And hold a final shape.

Try it once more, now: see if you can balance like that and add movements of your back. Now add back and shoulders. Now back, shoulders, arms, and head. Now slow motion. And hold your shape. Remember: keep those muscles tight.

Now imagine that you are inside a mirror. If I move my right arm like this, what does the image in my mirror do? It moves exactly with me, does just what I do. Try it: watch what I do, and do exactly the same thing. *(Go to a child who is following properly.)* I'll move slow motion so you can follow me exactly, just like a mirror. Watch which part of my body I'm moving. *(Move head, shoulders, arms, hands, etc., stepping or going from side to side, but never turning.)*

Now who wants to lead all the people in the mirror? *(Choose one child.)* Remember to go slowly. Good. You choose someone else now, and go back inside the mirror. *(Continue until all understand how to follow.)*

Now everyone choose a partner. Decide who will be the leader and who will be the mirror. Leaders, you move. See if you can move slowly and clearly so that your mirror can follow exactly. Ready, shape, begin.

Let's change leaders. Whoever was in the mirror come out and be the leader. Whoever was the leader, jump inside the mirror. This time, reach out and touch hands slowly. Now draw back slowly. Reach out and touch elbows. Draw back. Can you change level? How else do you like to move with your mirror? How many different shapes can your mirror follow exactly? Move your whole body. Now isolate one part, and see if your mirror can follow you.

Shall we watch these duets? Decide who will be the leader this time and who will be the mirror. Audience, watch to see if the leaders and mirrors can isolate different parts of their bodies. *(Performance and comments.)* Next group.

For our good-bye dance today, I want to see separate body parts moving. When you skip, try turning your head. Gallop and shake your hands. Combine a step and a body part. *(Play music.)*

Goals for evaluation: Watch that leaders move slowly, with sustained flow, and aim always for variety.

"Stretch, stretch." Most children have found a forward or sideward stretch at high level, but a girl in the center is stretching at low level, and one almost hidden is trying a backward stretch.

element: body moves

helper: rhythmic words

I'm going to say: stretch, stretch, bend, bend, bend. You make your body do what the words say. Ready, stretch, stretch, bend, bend, bend. Now let me see a stretch that isn't just a shape, but a stretch that moves. Try it first with your arms. Move out away from your body. Ready, stretch, stretch.

Can you do a middle level stretching move? Try it. Stretch, stretch. How about low level? Take a bent shape at low level, and stretch slowly out away from your center. S-t-r-e-t-c-h. Now let me see you change level as your stretch. Go. S-t-r-e-t-c-h. Now move through space; you can use any steps you want, but you must stretch as you go. Ready, go. Good.

Now move through space, bending as you go. I'll say: bend, bend, bend. Try hopping and bending. Go. Bend, bend, bend. Try jumping and bending. Bend, bend, bend.

All right, here we go again. I'll say: stretch, stretch, bend, bend, bend. This time you must change level, and you must change your place in the room. See how interesting you can make it. Ready, stretch, stretch, bend, bend, bend. Let's watch each other one at a time to see how many different ways you can do it. Stretch, stretch, bend, bend, bend. *(Continue until all have done it.)*

Now I'm going to add "twist," and you must make the longest, smoothest, tightest twisting move you can with your whole body so that when you finish you look like a pretzel! Ready, t-w-i-s-t. What is the difference between a twist and a bend? A twist must turn at the joints. Let me see that again, and be sure you are twisting not bending. Ready,

"Bend, bend, bend."

t-w-i-s-t. That's better. Now show me just one part of your body twisting. Now another. Now another. Now your whole body again.

Now show me a shaking movement with your whole body. Go. Stop. Show me a slow shake with your head. A fast shake with your hand. A slow shake with your whole body. And rest. Now try a vibratory shake—where you shake your arms or hand or leg without moving it through space. That's hard, isn't it? You have to tighten some muscles and release others. Can anyone do it?

"Twist."

Now we are ready for a word dance. The words will be: stretch, stretch, bend, bend, bend, t-w-i-s-t, shake; stretch, stretch, bend, bend, bend, t-w-i-s-t, shake. I must see a change of level and a change of place. Ready, go. Stretch, stretch, bend, bend, bend, t-w-i-s-t, shake. *(Repeat about five times.)*

Tell me: do you have to dance with your whole body at all times? No, you can isolate and use just a part. That will make it more interesting. Do you have to move in the same way each time you do it? No. Change it every time. See how many ways your body can do those moves.

Let's try it again, with just half the class at a time. Others sit where you are. Ready, stretch, stretch, bend, bend, bend, t-w-i-s-t, shake. *(If you have percussion instruments handy, let the children decide which instrument would best accompany each move, and have some watchers accompany the dancers. Since you have set the rhythm with your words, this is an easy way for children to experiment with the instruments.)*

In our good-bye dance today, be sure to include four different kinds of body moves. Exaggerate the differences. Make me see the different moves you can do. *(Play music.)*

Goals for evaluation: Check whether the children still challenge their muscles and their ability to balance. Look for ability to concentrate for a whole lesson.

element: rise and collapse

helper: TV act

Stretch your right arm high above your head. Really stretch, feel the tension in the muscles. When I say go, I want you to let your arm collapse. Go. What do you know that collapses like that? What does that word mean? This time, let your head and torso rise, then collapse until you are on the floor. Go.

What is the difference between a collapse and a bend? A collapse is a letting go, letting the air out, relaxing, dropping, giving in to gravity. This time I want you to collapse without bending through space. Try not to bend forward or backward or sideward. Just let your body sink from inside. You might feel tired, or you might think of letting your skin wrinkle at your waist. Remember, a collapse always goes straight downward. Try it. Go.

Let me see you rise and collapse and then stretch out to a prone position on the floor. Go. Let me see you rise and collapse and then stretch out to your right side. Land with your head over to your right side and your feet approximately where they are. Go. Rise and then collapse and stretch backward so that you end up lying on your back. Can you do that? Go.

Now try those directional falls by bending your body to get there. No collapsing this time. Ready, front fall. How can you do it? Side fall. Back fall. Is it possible to reach the floor *without* bending? How would you do it? Try it.

Show me any kind of fall—collapse, bend, or stretch—but use a turn on the way down. Go.

Now I'll count to three. On three, rise to the highest stretch you

"A collapse is a letting go, letting the air out, relaxing,
dropping, giving in to gravity."

can hold. Then imagine you're on TV. You're an actor who has to do a slow-motion death scene in a western. You've seen that, haven't you? Whoever falls with the slowest, most dramatic collapsed movement gets the part. Ready, one, two, three. Really let go. I must see the letting go in the center of your body. It's not the same as bending. Try it again. Don't think or plan what you'll do. Just let it happen. Turns and good shapes will happen if your mind is truly on the collapse. One, two, three.

Get back up from your spot, and this time take a walk, a run, a leap, or a skip to the high rise. Hold it just a second, and then collapse. I'll give you a crash on the drum just before your collapse. Ready, go.

Using the collapse in a TV act—a slow-motion death scene in a western.
Watching a few at a time helps children observe the variety in each other's movements.
Here the watchers can see different uses of head direction, body shape, and tempo.

Let's watch these collapses one *(or "a few")* at a time, and see who will get the TV part. Remember, you want to make this a slow, beautiful, collapsed, death scene. Use only enough tension to hold back the speed so that it is slow motion. It's hard to collapse in slow motion and keep it a collapse. Here we go. *(Continue until all have had a turn.)*

Goals for evaluation: Look for a dramatic flair, as well as for an understanding of collapse.

elements: swing, sway, circle

helper: moving playground

We've worked on stretching, bending, twisting, shaking, lifting, and collapsing. Today I want to see a swinging movement. What is a swinging motion? Swing your arms, back and forward. From side to side. Swing them using a large amount of space, a big swing. Now show me a small swing. What other parts of your body can swing? Your hand. Your leg. Your head? Yes, if you drop it forward. Your trunk? Yes, if you drop that forward too. Why must you drop your head or your trunk? Because a swing is like a pendulum or a playground swing. It's the bottom part of a circle; the fulcrum—the center or fastening—is at the top of the swinging bone, at the joint.

Make a full circle with your arms. The shoulder joint is in the middle of that circle. Make a full circle with your hand. Your head. Your ribs. Your hips. Your leg. Your lower leg. Your foot. Now do a swing again. A swing, remember, is the bottom part of a circle.

What else is characteristic about a swing? Swing your arms again. Let them swing freely, with no tension. What do you notice? There is a hesitation at the top of each side before the movement falls again. Now find another shape, perhaps low level, or turn yourself upside down, and see what part of your body can swing. Because of the letting go, a swing is a little bit like a collapse isn't it? But in a swing, the momentum in the movement creates a lift again, and the movement becomes continuous.

Now try moving through space. Swing and let the swing pull you through space, or let it turn you. Try it with your arms. Head. Leg.

Come back to your spot on the floor, and do one swing with your arms. Now draw the top part of that circle with your arms. Go. Keep

The moving playground. The center boy is starting an overhead sway; the boy on the right, an underhand swing; the girl on the left a sway with a leap. Can you tell which of the others are swinging and which are swaying?

drawing the top part of that circle back and forth, back and forth. What kind of movement are you doing? Yes, swaying. What do you know that sways? What other parts of your body can sway? Sway with your head. Your whole body. Your legs. Change level and shape; now what can sway? Try moving through space, walking and swaying. Let the sway turn you. Feel the sway as part of a horizontal circle. Can you feel the difference between swinging and swaying? Sway is back and forth; swing feels more like up and down.

All come over and sit by me. Let's take the idea of a playground—a

"How far can your body sway?"

moving playground. Everything on this playground must swing or sway or circle. What is the first thing you could put on this playground? Swings. Can you make your body swing through space like a real swing? Good. What else? Trees; they sway. A seesaw sways. A baseball pitcher; his arm circles, he pitches underhand and throws overhand—lots of swings and sways there! What else? Wind sways and circles. A tether ball swings and circles. What else?

Now decide what part of this moving playground you want to be. If you can't decide, be yourself and experiment with the movement. Make a swing or sway or circle that no one else has seen before. There's plenty of room for people on this playground. Ready, show me your starting shape, go. And hold your ending shape. Now let's watch each other in groups. *(Performance and comments.)*

Goals for evaluation: Look for total body movement and free use of open space.

element: big and little

helper: land of the giants

Make the biggest high level shape you can. Make the biggest low level shape you can. I'm going to count to ten, and I want you to move through the biggest amount of space you can by the time I say ten. Ready, one *(count through),* ten.

This time use big movements while you are traveling through a large amount of space. Remember to use low space as well as high space. Ready, go. One *(count through),* ten.

Is it possible to make a big movement with a small part of your body? Now how about trying a small movement with your back. Your leg. Now cup your hands together and make a small packet of space. Put your thumb into that space and make the smallest move you can in the smallest amount of space. Go. Can you make a movement that small with your shoulders? Your hand? Your head? Your foot?

As I beat the drum, show me big movements. When I beat the rim, show me small movements. Go anywhere you want to travel in space. Ready, go.

What can you do to make me notice your small movements? The shape you are holding helps. Your focus helps. This time, when you make a small movement, make it show. Look at it; make your whole body shape focus on it. Go.

Now let's think about steps. Show me big walks. Tiny walks. Do you all have to walk forward? Show me sideward or backward or circling walks. What about a small body shape to go with a small walk? Skip big. Skip small. Gallop big. Gallop small. Can you gallop with your fingers? Arms? Big and small? Now start with a small movement and make it

"Use big movements, and travel through a large amount of space."
Most children think of big as high level, and they have to be
challenged to use big moves at low level.

"When you make a small movement, make it show." The girl in the foreground
is using focus and shape to direct attention to small finger moves.

bigger and bigger. Go. Do the opposite: start with a big movement and get smaller and smaller. Try it.

Get into small groups *(or "partners")*. Make a dance that shows contrast in size. Show me "Land of the Giants." I must see huge giants, and I must see tiny little people and insects. How many different kinds of moves will the giants think of? What will the tiny people do? Maybe they'll surprise us and grow bigger! Decide what you'll do. We'll go over it once together. Then I'll let you practice two minutes, and then we'll watch.

Ready, everyone in a starting shape. Go. I must know right away if you're big or little. Show me contrast in levels, perhaps. Make it an interesting group shape. Now move. And make an ending shape.

Practice by yourselves now for two minutes. Especially practice your ending shapes. Remember: starting shape, movements, ending shape. *(Watch and comment.)*

Goals for evaluation: Check whether the children have ideas when they get together. Look for enthusiasm and challenge.

element: sharp and smooth

helper: instruments

Today we're going to get into our racing cars and onto the racetrack. As I beat the drum, you go around the room as fast as you can. When I stop, put on your brakes and stop as suddenly as you can. Ready, go. Stop. Let's try that again. No slowing down, just a sudden stop. Ready, go. Stop!

Tell me: what does your body have to do to stop? *(Answers have been: jump into the floor, pull back, bend your knees, tighten your muscles. Try each method, and see whether each helps.)*

Now I'll play a certain number of beats on the drum, so that you can anticipate the stop and control it. I'll play four beats. Stop on "four." Stop sharply! Ready, one, two, three, four. One, two, three, four. *(Do several times.)*

Now I want you to move and stop on every beat. You'll have no time to move through space, so just stay right on your spot and move sharply. Ready, stop, stop, stop, stop. Think only of the sudden stop. Stop as soon as you start. Try your head alone. Go. Sharp, sharp, sharp, sharp. Now your shoulders. Now your back. Move, move, move, move. Don't let it get smooth. Now your arms. Now try your whole body at once. Stop, stop, stop, stop. You are moving sharply.

Come over to me. Tell me: what is a sharp movement? *(Answers have been: angular, fast, short, tight, pointed, direct, hard. Have the children try to do the opposite of each answer sharply to discover what really makes sharp movement. I stress that the stopping is the most important aspect.)*

I am going to play a sound that has no stop. Move with this sound as long as you can hear it. *(Play triangle, gong, or cymbals.)* This is a

The seated girl is playing an instrument with a sharp sound, probably a woodblock. The children are making sharp moves as she plays. When the girl with the triangle plays, the movement will be smooth, to match the sound. The seated boys have instruments too. The instruments are played one at a time.

lasting, smooth sound. It has no sharp stops in it. Try it again, and see if you can move continuously. Sustain the movement. Try changing your level, rolling and standing and moving through space with a free-flowing movement, and never stopping. Keep your movement smooth—no change in force and no stops. Ready, go. Move until the sound dies away, and when you can hear it no longer hold your final shape.

Let's sit in a circle now, and take turns playing the triangle. You can get sharp sounds that stop by deadening the vibration with your hand. You get a smooth ongoing sound by hanging it from a string or rubber band. As each person plays, dance with part of your body right here in the circle. We'll move the way they play, either sharply or smoothly. *(Continue with other instruments, if available, such as claves, woodblocks, guiros, gongs, or cymbals.)*

Is it possible to do steps smoothly and sharply? Try skips. Do four smooth and four sharp. Go. Smooth, smooth, smooth, smooth, sharp, sharp, sharp, sharp. Do gallops. Jumps. Hops. Walks. Leaps.

Now move across the floor any way you wish, but doing four counts smooth and four counts sharp. Go. Show me contrast.

Get a partner. One of you be Mr. or Ms. Smooth, and one of you be Mr. or Ms. Sharp. Get a starting shape. Make sure I can see a smooth shape and a sharp shape. What makes a smooth shape? We talked about movements, but not about shapes. What makes a sharp shape? Now do some movements. Make an ending shape. Practice and we'll watch them in two minutes. Go. *(Watch and comment with the children. Comments are drawn from this lesson and all previous lessons.)*

Goals for evaluation: Look for good use of crossovers and variety. Look for sharp movements that are large and explosive, for smooth moves that reach into space.

A fast–slow quartet. The three slow movers
are changing level and staying on one spot, while
the fast mover is moving through space.

element: fast and slow

helper: paint with your body

When I say go, I want you to move your whole body as fast as you can and stop when I say stop. Ready, go, stop. *(Wait only a second between the two instructions; most of the children will hardly have begun.)* Do it again. Ready, go, stop. This time move not just your feet, but every part of your body: your hands, head, eyelashes, nose, shoulders, hips, back, legs. Ready, go. Stop.

Next, I want you to move as slowly as it is possible for a person to move. Ready, shape, go. Move so that it barely shows, but so that it doesn't stop. How slowly can you move? Can you change your level? How slowly can you roll? Crawl? Walk? Gallop? Skip? Run? Collapse? Shake?

Let me see you do a fast—slow dance now. I won't beat for you this time because you will decide when you will move fast and when you will move slowly. Don't worry about what the other people are doing. If they are moving fast, you might be moving slowly. In fact, try to be different from those around you. Feel the contrast between you and others. Change whenever you want to. No one must move at medium tempo—only very fast or very slow. Move in the extremes of slow and fast. Ready, go.

Now we are going to paint the air with our bodies. Think of big, slow strokes of paint through the space and fast splashes too. Think of spurts and dashes as well as fine, thin, slow, careful lines. Imagine using different colors, and paint a beautiful, exciting, massive picture in this room. Ready, go. Remember, your whole body is the paintbrush, so you can lead the movement with different parts of your body. Paint with your head, your knee, your back, your elbows. Paint with your whole self. Paint with red, blue, black, yellow. Make wide strokes fast and wide strokes slowly. Cover the space slowly, then fast. Throw darts of color into different directions. How many ways can you think of to spread color in this room? And make an ending shape.

Now let's talk about acceleration and retardation—speeding up and slowing down. Let's do just what the words say: we'll speed up and slow down. Start low level and go up as you make your movements faster. Then when you are as high as you can hold, gradually slow down and lower the level. Ready, go. Start very slowly so you can increase your speed. Hold your shape at the end. I'll wait for everyone.

Now let's move across the floor. Accelerate. Ready, go. Retard. Ready, go.

Get partners for a fast—slow dance. You can be a couple of characters or a thing or yourselves or you can paint the space. Whatever you do, it must be a fast—slow dance. Make the change of tempo the most interesting thing about your duet. How many ways can you show contrast between fast and slow? Get a beginning shape and practice. Beginning shape, movements, ending shape. When you are ready, come sit by me, and we'll watch. *(Performance and comments.)*

Goals for evaluation: Stress doing large, fast moves; they are hard to do and take energy!

element: tight and loose

helper: spaghetti monsters

(Show the children a small package wrapped tightly with string, and then some loose string—or any other examples of tight and loose.) Tell me the difference between the string on the package and the other piece of string. Yes, one is tight and one is loose. One is straight, the other is curved. Can you make your body tight like the string that is tight on the package? Show me. What happens to your muscles? Can you move like that? Can you move your arms as if they were wrapping a package very tightly? It's a big package, and your arms wrap it very, very tightly. Can you keep those arms tight and stretch out away from your package? Can you make your legs move tightly like that? Your muscles are hard, and the movement is bound like the package. Can you change your level with tight muscles? Can you move your back like that? Skip? Jump?

Now this other piece of string: look how it flops, how loose it is. Can you make your body loose and floppy like that? Show me. Can you skip loosely and floppily? Jump? Hop? Can you change level? Can you move your back like that?

Who likes spaghetti? What is spaghetti like before it is cooked? Show me. Straight and hard. And then what happens when it is cooked? It gets loose and very floppy.

Once upon a time there were some pieces of spaghetti, and I thought to myself: "I think I'll have some spaghetti for supper." So I put the long, straight pieces into the boiling water and watched. What happened? Look at those stiff bodies gradually become limp and loose!

Then, to my surprise, the spaghetti started to dance to the music of

The monsters on the right with tight muscles are attacking the
loose-muscled spaghetti on the left. The front left boy is using a
collapsed move, while the boy behind him is using bends and hopping.
Most of the aggressors are using forward walks with body shapes.
One barely visible at the far right is approaching at middle level.

the boiling water—a loose, floppy dance, with jumps, and turns, and levels, and all parts of its body moving.

Just then a huge monster who loved spaghetti came in, with big, tight movements. He could twist, bend, stretch, but only in a tight, bound way—only with very tight muscles. He could move his back and his legs and change level and crawl, but only tight, tight, tight. Suddenly he saw the dancing spaghetti. What happened? *(Let the children finish the story!)*

Today in your good-bye dance I want to see two things. What do you suppose those two elements are? Yes, tight and loose: tight, bound movements and loose, floppy movements. *(Play music. Percussion music is good because it suits both tight and loose movements.)*

Goals for evaluation: See whether the children can dance such a silly story and still use their energy clearly. Energy must be used in the extreme to be clear.

Finding strong
movement. The
girl is pressing
apart with her
arms, the boy on
the right is lifting
a weight with
his back, and the
boy on the left is
pulling a weight.

element: heavy and light

helper: no noise

Pound on the floor as hard as you want to with your fist once. Go. Now do it again, but don't touch the floor; just feel the strength in your movement, without the noise. Do it sharply. Go. Remember, sharp means with a sudden stop. Try it again. Go. Now do it smoothly, but with just as much weight behind it. Go. Keep that weight moving evenly. Do it again with the other hand. Press downward heavily. Go.

Now with either hand, let your fist float lightly down to the floor. Your other hand. Lightly to the floor. Keep the shape of the fist if you can, so that we are not making strong and light shapes, only strong and light movements. Ready, go. Lightly. Can you do that movement sharply but lightly? Try it.

Now lift something upward above your head with strong force. Imagine a very heavy weight. Lift it with your arms. Lift it with your legs. Lift it with your back. Lift it with your shoulders.

Now just the opposite. Lift something light as air above your head. Lift it slowly but lightly. Lift it quickly. Lift it with your arms. Your legs. Your shoulders. Your back.

Push something heavy away from you. Push it with your back. Your arms. Your whole body. Now flick something lightly away from you. Use a small amount of space and press. Use a large amount of space and press. Pull something of great weight. Do that very same motion very lightly.

Now do all the strong movements you can think of. Think of strong movement as movement with weight behind it or weight in front of it. Your body is heavy and the air is heavy. Go. Make me feel the

Finding light movement.
The boy is floating downward
with the whole body.

weight and see the strength it takes to move it. Do some skips and jumps and leaps with strength and weight. Try changing level. Keep the feeling of strength. Remember to hold back the weight so that no noise happens.

Now do just the opposite: lightness. Skipping. Jumping. No noise! Galloping. Everyone listen, and let's see who can gallop the most quietly.

For the good-bye dance, let me see all lightness. Lots of quick darts and dodges, leaps, skips, jumps, turns, and gallops. Then, suddenly at the end, just before your ending shape, do a great strong movement ending with a great strong shape. *(Play music.)*

Goals for evaluation: Look for the ability to change from light to heavy and keep the shapes and steps varied.

"Look at something in the room with your whole body."

element: focus

helper: haunted house

When you are talking to someone, as I'm talking to you now, what part of that person do you look at? The face. When people watch dancers, they watch their faces as much as any other part of their bodies. Have you ever tried to make someone look at something in the distance? *(Point and look behind the children to get them to turn and look too.)* The part of the face that we're going to talk about today is the eyes. We call the use of the eyes *focus.* In dance when we use focus, we use the whole body to help the eyes. Just now when I pointed, I used my arm and hand to help my eyes show you the focus.

I'm going to say ready, get set, go. On go, focus on something in this room: the wall, the floor, the ceiling, the clock, anything. Ready, get set, go. Again. Ready, get set, go. This time I want you to make the shape of your body exaggerate the focus, help the focus. Make us all want to look where you are looking. Ready, get set, go. Ready, get set, go. Ready, get set, go.

Those were fast, sharp changes. Now show me a slow, smooth change of focus. Take three counts, and sneak your eyes and your shape to another point in the room. Ready, one, two, three. Again. One, two, three.

Let's line up on one side of the room. We'll all go across the room at once. First, when I say go, run across the room, changing your focus as you go. Look behind you, at the floor, at the ceiling, at your watch. Where else can you think to surprise us and look? Ready, all together, go.

This time I want you to crawl halfway across the room looking for something. It might be on the floor, or somewhere else—who knows?

When you get halfway, find it, jump up, and run the rest of the way. But while you're running, show me by your focus that someone is chasing you. Ready, go.

Now come back to a spot in the room. Sometimes when dancers don't know what to do with their eyes, they end up looking at another person and lose their concentration. Move around through space with each other now, but keep your eyes on your hands. Let your hands lead the movement and follow with your eyes. Go. This time as you move, focus on the ceiling or walls. Go. This time try focusing on the air — on the space itself. Go. Okay. Remember: your eyes should always be part of your dancing, focusing on something, not breaking your concentration.

Listen to these words: focus, step, isolation, level. When I say the word, you must do it. Focus — look at some point with your whole body helping your eyes. Step — move about three or four steps through space. Your step could be a jump, walk, crawl, anything. Let's do that much again. Ready, focus, step. Focus, step.

Now let's add isolation. That means only one part of your body moves, everything else freezes. Ready, isolation. Show me another part, perhaps your head or your hand or your foot, something I don't expect. Ready, isolation.

And now change level. You can go down if you are up or up if you are down. You can go down, up, down, or change as many times as you wish. Ready, level.

Now listen to the tempo in which I'll say the words. Focus, step, isolation, level. Ready, begin. Focus, step, isolation, level. Good. Let's do it again and again, until you remember what comes next. Focus, step, isolation, level. *(Etc.)*

Let's see if you can do something else. Imagine you are in a haunted house. No one is there saying focus, step, isolation, level. You must keep the order of things just like that, but since I am not going to be saying those words, you can continue any one of them as long as you wish, but you must do first focus, then step, then isolation, then level. Because the duration—the length of time—of each step will be up to you, that means that all of you will not be doing the same thing at the same time. You might be moving more slowly and may only be up to isolation when someone else is at level. Do you think you can concentrate and keep going anyway?

Let's try it. I'll play some haunted house music. Keep going until the music stops. Remember, your focus must be strong and clear. Never focus on another dancer. It might break his or her concentration. Ready, here we go. *(Play music.)*

Goals for evaluation: Watch to see if the children can sustain the use of focus throughout their dance, even while they are doing step, isolation, and level. Can they go from one focus to another without breaking concentration? Do their whole bodies enhance their focus?

Finding straight lines in the body and straight paths
through space. "Imagine you are downtown
where all the streets are straight."

element: pathways

helper: writing in space

Today I want you to imagine you are downtown where all the streets are straight. Stand up and face one of the walls. I'll beat four times, and you walk straight toward that wall four steps. Suppose you see you might bump into someone—remember: dancers never bump. What can you do? That's right. You can walk backwards. What else? Walk in place until the other person passes. But do not turn. Ready, one, two, three, four. Now face a different wall, and do four more steps. Ready, one, two, three, four. And a different wall. *(Count.)* Good. Feel how square and straight everything is. No turns, only sharp changes of direction. This time I won't stop. I'll keep playing even beats and you keep walking in straight lines. You can walk as many steps in one direction as you wish. Make sharp changes in direction. Feel straight and tall. Ready, go.

Now let's form a circle. Hold hands to form the circle. Now drop hands, and take one step backward to make the circle a little larger. Face so that your left shoulder is toward the center and let's walk around the circle. Go. And stop. What happens to the circle? It gets smaller. Why? Because everyone leans in slightly. When we make a circular path through space, our bodies do the same thing they do when we turn a corner on a bicycle. What do you do on a bicycle? You lean, that's right. Same thing happens when an airplane turns—it banks. Road builders bank the turns on a roadway to make it safer for cars to turn.

Let's walk around again, and this time feel your body leaning in a little. Ready, go. Now reverse, and let's walk around in the other direction in a circle. Go. Now you are leaning in with the other side of your body.

Making curved lines in the body and a curved path through space. Some of the children are imagining they are driving on a banked roadway.

Walk anywhere in the room you wish, but this time make curved pathways rather than straight lines. You make curves and turns by leaning. Everyone make a figure eight by leaning. Go. Let your body fall as it goes. Let the feel of the curve take over. Now, go anywhere you want to go, change from leaning right to leaning left, and let your body just go. Be surprised where it leads you. Ready, go.

Now when I beat the rim, make curved lines. When I beat the head of the drum, make straight lines. Feel the change in your body. Ready, rim. Head. Rim. Head.

Everyone come to one side of the room and spread out all along the wall. I am going to write my name on the floor with my feet as I walk. Watch me and tell me if I am printing in straight lines or if I am writing in curved lines. *(I write Mary.)*

You write your name, or print it. Let's have four people *(or as many as can move freely)* go at once. As soon as there is room, the next person start. Watch to see if you can see the name being spelled out. Go.

Line up back at the wall again. I want you to take your favorite letter from your name, and this time use the whole room for that one letter. You can write it by leaps, skips, jumps, any steps, but show me where it is curved and where it is straight. Let's have the first four start. When your letter ends, hold a low shape on the floor. Next people start whenever there is room.

Today for our good-bye dance I want to see a combination of curved and straight pathways through the space. *(Play music.)*

Goals for evaluation: See that the children truly understand and feel centrifugal force in their curving pathways.

Finding free-flowing movement—movement that has no thought of stopping. Running, twirling, and swinging are often discovered as having a free-flowing quality.

element: free flow, bound flow, and balance

helper: stillness

Today instead of moving, we're going to concentrate on its opposite. What is the opposite of moving? Stopping. This time don't wait for me to stop you by stopping my drum, I want you to find how exciting it is to stop on your own, even when no one else stops. Go anywhere in the room, with the music, putting in stops whenever you like. Go. *(Play lively music.)*

What makes an interesting stop? Shape, yes. This time when you stop, stop in a shape that is like a sculpture—interesting to look at from all sides. Stop for as short or as long a time as you like. Start to feel what it's like to stop when others are moving around you. Feel what it's like to move when others have stopped. Go.

Let's forget stopping for a minute and think about free-flowing movement—movement that has no thought of stopping, where the body just soars through space. You should feel that you are in a perpetual motion machine. Feel the air moving past you at all times. Go. Run through the room and feel the air move past your face. Keep the forward pressure even, and go fast enough so that you can tell me the temperature of the air. Go. What is the temperature? Do it again. Now walk as slowly as you can and still move with enough pressure to feel the air pass by you.

Move in that same free-flowing way, but change your level. Sit and roll and spin but keep moving, finding the momentum that will bring you to standing and running or skipping again. Go.

Now sit on the floor and combine free-flowing movement and stillness with just your arms. Move your arms freely, feeling the air passing, then stop and hold till the air is quiet. Feel as you move that you are churning the air. Go. This time move your arms in the same pathways, but feel as if you are pushing them through heavy water. Your arms are no longer free. The movement is bound. Now add stops to that bound movement—short stops and short moves. Make it jerky. The movement along the pathway is bound.

Combine free-flowing and bound movements now with your whole body through space. This time add balance. Try to be still at some very unusual or difficult point, such as halfway down to low level, or on one knee, or high on one foot, or halfway through a roll on the floor. Make the balance as exciting as the movement. Hold the balance as long as you can. Feel your whole body and the air become still and quiet. I won't play any accompaniment because you need to establish your own rhythm for this. Go.

That was beautiful. Let's watch half the class at a time.

For our good-bye dance, let's combine free-flowing movement, bound movement, and balance, using a musical background. Feel what it's like to move freely, to move in a bound way, and then to hold a balance while the music still moves. *(Some soaring movie background music is good here.)*

Goals for evaluation: Look for large use of space. This kind of spontaneous movement should feel good: watch for signs that the children are enjoying it. Their movements should show increases in range and variety.

element: accent

helper: names

I'm going to hum "Pop Goes the Weasel." When I say pop, make your biggest shape. *(Hum.)* Let's do that again. Dance any way you wish while I hum, then make sure the "pop" shows. *(Hum.)*

Now come to me, making a move each time I say pop. Pop goes the weasel, pop goes the weasel *(etc.)*. Imagine you are clowns approaching. Show me crazy shapes; make me laugh as you approach. Pop goes the weasel, pop goes the weasel *(etc.)*.

Listen to this sentence: *Give* me the bag. Someone say it accenting a different word. Give *me* the bag. Give me *the* bag. Give me the *bag*. What does accent mean? Louder, stronger, longer, sharper.

How many sounds are in that sentence? Four. Let's say it and clap it. *(Do it without any accent.)* Give me the bag. Now dance it with your feet. Accent the word "bag." Go. Instead of all walks, this time put in a jump. Now put in a hop. Can you add a turn? Can you change your level? Give me the *bag,* give me the *bag.* Can you dance it not with your feet but with your body? This time let's accent the word "give." *Give* me the bag, *give* me the bag. How many movements are you doing in all? Four. Which one is accented? The first. Let's do it with our bodies and our feet, over and over again. *Give* me the bag, *give* me the bag *(etc.)*.

When we dance, just as when we speak, we use accents to add interest and force to what we dance. We don't speak in a monotone—all words even, all the same—nor do we dance that way. Remember when we worked with heartbeat? That was an even beat. Listen. *(Beat the drum or clap evenly.)* Let's walk to this beat. Now accent the first of every four beats. *One,* two, three, four, *one,* two, three, four *(etc.)*. Show me the

Four children introducing themselves by dancing the accent of
their names. Each holds his last shape until all have finished. All these
here have used sharp, bent moves and shapes. Angular, direct,
small moves are the clearest to give accent.

accent by moving your head, but keep the beat going in your feet. *One, two, three, four.*

Now accent the first of every three beats. *One,* two, three, *one,* two, three. This time accent the beat or make it stronger by adding a movement with your shoulders. Go. Now accent one of every five. Accent with your back. That's harder, isn't it? A five beat is not so easy. *One,* two, three, four, five *(etc.).* Accent one of every two. *One,* two, *one,* two. Accent with your elbows.

In movement, what makes an accent? Using a different part of your body, changing direction. This time, on the first of every four beats, change your direction. This time on the first of every four beats, change your level. This time on the first of every four beats accent any way you wish. What can your body do to make the accent show? Focus—can you accent with focus? A hop? A stamp? A clap? Level? Direction? What else can you think of?

Come sit in a circle. My name is Mary *(use your name).* How many sounds is that? How many syllables? Which one do you hear the strongest? Clap my name. What's your name? *(Go around the circle, all clapping names and deciding on accents.)*

Now everyone stand up and dance your own name with your feet only. Next add a body movement on the accent only. Practice. We'll go around the room, and you introduce yourself by saying your name as you dance it.

Let's all say happy new year *(or some other appropriate phrase).* Let's decide which syllable is accented. Everyone find a way to dance it that covers space and uses a variety of steps. Let's dance it over and over.

Now we'll do these phrases one at a time as our good-bye dances. Everybody say it while the dancer dances it. I'll beat it on my drum. Let's see how much variety in shapes and steps we can manage.

Goals for evaluation: Look for clarity in small moves.

Clapping whole, half, and quarter notes. When the children have
learned the duration of each, the pieces of paper can be laid out
in any order to form a rhythmic pattern. Children enjoy making
designs with the papers and then clapping the pattern produced.

element: duration

helper: quarter, half, whole

(Bring to class one piece of construction paper whole, a second piece cut in half, and a third piece cut into quarters (strips). Bring two such sets to demonstrate two whole notes, four half notes, and eight quarter notes.) *

Here is a whole piece of paper. If I cut it in half, how many pieces would I have? Two. Here they are. If I cut that same whole piece of paper into quarters, how many would I have? Four. Here they are. The names of notes in music or beats in dance are the same as the names for those pieces of paper: whole, half, and quarter—like a whole dollar, a half dollar, and a quarter.

If I played four quarter notes on my drum it would sound like this. *(Beat four times.)* The whole note I would beat just once because there is just one piece of paper, but it would last for four beats like the four quarters. Listen. *(Play the triangle, and deaden it after four beats.)* Someone clap four quarter notes while I play a whole note on the triangle. Ready, beat.

Who thinks he or she could fit two half notes into those four beats? You have only two sounds, or two claps because there are only two pieces of paper there. Clap: one, hold, three, hold. Clap at the beginning of the sound. Let's all clap whole notes. My triangle will last the four beats; your clap will last inside our heads. Ready, go. One, hold, hold, hold, one, hold, hold, hold. Now let's beat half notes. Ready, one, hold,

---

*The ideas in this lesson were originated by Virginia Tanner of the Children's Dance Section, University of Utah Extension Division, who was the inspiration of many teachers of children's dance.

one, hold, one, hold, one, hold. Now let's beat quarter notes: one, one, one, one, one, one, one, one.

Now I'm going to add another whole set. First, another whole note. How many half notes equal that? Two. How many quarter notes? Four. Let's clap just what we see. First, the top row—the two whole notes. Ready, clap, hold, hold, hold, clap, hold, hold, hold. Now the second row—the four half notes. Ready, clap, hold, clap, hold, clap, hold, clap, hold. Now the third row—the quarter notes. Ready, clap, clap, clap, clap, clap, clap, clap, clap.

Let's do all three rows at the same time. Who wants to clap whole notes? Half notes? Quarter notes? Ready, go.

Now we are going to move with each note. First, let's all move with the long whole note. I'll play the triangle, and you make the movement long and smooth. Keep it going for four beats. Just one move, but keep it going for four counts. Ready, and one. Now let's move two whole notes. Ready, and one, two.

Next let's move with four half notes. Each movement lasts two beats. Ready, one, hold, two, hold, three, hold, four, hold. Let's do that again. One, two, three, four, five, six, seven, eight. Why did I count eight?

Let's have this half of the room move with two whole notes, and the other half with four half notes. We should come out even, shouldn't we? Ready, and one *(count through)*, eight.

Now let's do the quarter notes. Try sharp bending movements for these notes so that we shall see each move on each beat. Ready, and one *(count through)*, eight.

Shall we try putting all three together? Let me have three people who think they can do it. Ready, one *(count through)*, eight.

Good. Each time we have four quarters, let's call that a measure. How many measures are here on the floor? Can you imagine four measures? Let's clap four measures: first group you be wholes, second group be halves, third group be quarters, and let's all clap at once. Four measures. How many wholes is that? Four. How many halves? Eight. How many quarters? Sixteen. Ready, and one *(count through)*, sixteen.

Now let's make groups of three people. One be a quarter, one be a half, and one be a whole. See if you can dance four measures and come out even. The person who is the whole note will count out loud for the others. Dancers count like this: one, two, three four; two, two, three, four; three, two, three, four; four, two, three, four. Can you do that? Practice. Then we'll watch each group.

Goals for evaluation: Look for clear mathematical understanding.

"Beat the floor, your body, or the space. Use both your hands
and your feet, making rhythm patterns at different levels."
Using strongly rhythmic music and limiting the length of time
the children dance make this a challenge.

element: pattern

helper: leaving out, filling in

(Choose a piece of music that is rhythmically simple and clear and divided into phrases of eight beats—two measures of 4/4, or four measures of 2/4. Folk-dance music is good.)

Everyone clap to this music with me. *(Turn down the volume without removing the needle while you speak; then turn up the volume again for participation.)* Now let me have a turn clapping by myself for eight beats, then it will be your turn. Here we go with the music. My turn. Your turn. My turn. Your turn. *(Point to them at their turn. If you can count aloud at the same time, good.)*

This time listen to how I clap. I shall leave out some numbers. One, —, —, four, five, —, seven, eight. You can leave out any numbers you wish. Ready, here we go. My turn. Your turn. My turn. Your turn. *(Etc.)*

Next I'm going to fill in between the regular beats. Listen. One, and two, and a three, and a four a, and a five a, and six, and seven, and eight. *(Do whatever feels good to you.)* Now you fill in however you would like to. Ready, my turn. Your turn. *(Etc.)*

This time I will leave out some counts and fill in others. Listen. One, —, three, and four a, and a five, —, —, eight. Your turn. Do anything you like. My turn. Your turn. *(Etc.)*

This time, instead of just clapping, stand up and be free to turn and move, so that you can clap in a different spot in space each time, as if you're catching mosquitoes. Fill in and leave out wherever you wish. My turn first, for eight beats. Then your turn. Here we go.

This time imagine the floor is your drum, and make the rhythm with your feet. You can run, stamp, hop, jump—whatever feels good. Clap at the same time if you wish. No more turns for me—it's all yours now. Ready, go.

Let's do this again. See if you can change your level. Remember: keep clapping or making rhythm with your feet. Leave out more beats; the stops are interesting. Then put in lots of fast ones. You'll be making patterns in rhythm. Ready, go.

Now I'll change the music. This time see if you can make your own rhythm pattern to the music. Start in a shape. Ready, begin when you hear the music.

Shall we try some slow music? This may be harder. See if you can still make rhythm patterns. Use your hands, your feet, your whole body this time. Make your body moves uneven—sometimes long like a whole note, sometimes short. Make patterns in time.

This will be our good-bye dance. Which was your favorite record? All right, one at a time across the floor. Dance with the rhythm of your whole body.

Goals for evaluation: Look for the ability to let go, to let the rhythmic body take over.

elements: levels and tempo

helper: twins

When I say go, I want you to drop to the floor and hold your shape. Ready, get set, go. Let's do that again, and this time don't think about what your shape will be. Let it just happen. Get there fast. Ready, get set, go. Hold it. Now stay right there, and start to memorize your position. Where is your center of gravity? What parts of you are touching the floor? Which direction in the room are you facing? Can you remember this position exactly? Okay. Stand up and let's find it again. You must find the exact same position. Ready, get set, go. Have you got it? Good. Let's call this position 1. Stay right there. When I say go this time, find another low position—low level or middle level—but get there suddenly and without planning. Ready, get set, go. Stay there. Now memorize this position. This is position 2. Where is your center of weight now? Which way are you facing? Memorize the relationship of your body parts. Which parts are touching the floor? Now go back to position 1. Go to 2. To 1. To 2. Position 3 will be high level. Don't give me a plain standing position; find an interesting shape and hold it. Ready, get set, go.

Let's review: position 1, position 2, position 3, 2, 1, 3.

We've been going into each position with fast speed. Now I want you to find how slowly you can move into each position. It will be harder to do slowly. Find what you have to do to control the movement and hold your balance slowly. Ready, go. Into position 1. As soon as you are there, move into position 2. And as soon as you have position 2, rise to position 3. Don't worry if you're ahead of or behind someone else. If you get to 3 start down to 1 again. Feel your own moves. Are they smooth and slow? As slow as is humanly possible without stopping? Don't let your body stop. Don't let it fall or flop. Keep it controlled and smooth and slow and steady. *(Let the children continue until all have gone through the positions at least once.)*

All right. Now you have moved through all your positions fast, and you've moved through all your positions slowly. This time I want it all slow, very, very slow, except in one place, and that place must be very fast—excitingly fast! You can decide: do you want to drop into 1 fast and do the rest slowly? Or do you want to go from 1 to 2 fast and keep the rest very slow? Or do you want to shoot up at the end to 3 and do all the low levels slowly? You decide. Only one change can be fast. All the rest of your dance must be slow. Experiment. See how you'd like to do it. Ready, go. *(I sometimes do a dramatic series of beats on the drum, or play music that is not particularly metrical, such as electronic music or sound effects records.)*

Now let me see how you have decided to arrange your movements. All together. Use 3 as your starting position. Go through 1, 2, and 3, and then begin again. Do it over and over until I stop you. Make sure you do exactly the same thing again and again. Your eye and body focus must be clearly the same each time. Ready, go. *(If there is time, continue. If not, have them remember their level and speed pattern until the next meeting, and continue this lesson then.)*

Now find a partner. One of you be A and one of you be B. A's raise your hands. B's raise your hands. You are going to make a duet. First A will teach B his or her movements. When you can both do A's pattern, call me and let me see it. You must be able to do it without looking at each other. You must do it in unison, like twins, both facing the same direction in the room, *not* facing each other as we did in mirrors.

For instance, if I were going to learn Sally's first move, I would first watch her. I would stand either behind her or next to her like this and we would do it together. Then she would watch me to see if I do it exactly the way she does it. Finally, she would tell me whether she does her first move fast or slowly. If it's fast, we both do it as fast as possible. If it is

Three sets of "twins." The couple on the right is on the
way down to position 1, the center two have just come to position 3,
and those on the left are on their way up from position 2.

slow, we stay together both moving as slowly as possible. When we both can move into position 1 together like twins, then she teaches me position 2 and finally position 3. After A teaches B, then B will teach A, and you'll have a long duet. Let's try, and I'll come around to help you.

(This lesson is worth working on because the children learn how to learn movement. For the first time they are learning someone else's moves, not finding their own. When they are able to move as twins, have a few couples perform together with background music. This creates quite an exciting dance study in levels.)

Goals for evaluation: Look for the ability to see and learn movement.

element: review

helper: scarves

As I come around to you, tell me which color scarf you want. I'll put on some music, and you can dance with the scarf any way you want to. Ready, go. *(Folk tunes are good.)*

(Lower the volume to talk, but keep the music playing.) Now try holding the scarf in your other hand. Try changing hands. Try holding the scarf with your foot. Your elbow. Your head. Your back. Now let the scarf float by itself. Can you get under it? Let it fall, and go over it. How slowly can you go over it? Take a low level; how can you move the scarf now? And hold a shape.

Now that you know what you can do with the scarf, let me see you move with all the strength of your muscles, strongly and slowly. Can you make the scarf move with you in that way? Can you roll it? Twist it? Throw it? What can you do with the scarf to give the feeling of strength? *(Brass or percussion music at a slower tempo is good for this.)*

Now show me the feeling of riding on breath—both you and your scarf. Ready, go. *(Play soaring or lilting music.)* You can go anywhere in the space.

The next piece of music I'll play will be something you haven't heard before. Try a combination of breath and muscles. See how many different qualities you can get with that scarf. Don't forget to change level, direction, size, force, and flow. This time I shall play the record all the way through. It lasts about 2½ minutes. What can you do if you get tired? Think how you can keep dancing and still rest. Perhaps take a low level and move your fingers on the scarf. Perhaps let the scarf rest over

Dancing with props that move (balloons, balls, hula hoops, scarves) can increase concentration by providing an added challenge.

your face as you sway. Try not to stop dancing. Try to keep the feeling going until the music ends. Want to try? Who thinks he or she can last the whole record? Here we go. And end.

What is it like to dance with a scarf? Now look at the color of your scarf. Show me how that color makes you feel. First without the scarf. Begin. Trade scarves with a friend. How would you dance that color? Trade again. You can imagine your scarf to be anything. What is it? Does it make you want to use lots of space or very small space? Does it lead to free-flowing movements or stillness?

Let's watch. First all the red scarves. *(Etc.)*

Our good-bye dance will be all the freedom and variety in movement that you can do. Move with your mind, your body, and your spirit, using all the elements of dance! When you make your final shape, fold your scarf and put it into the scarf box using dance movements.

(This lesson can be simplified for use with the younger children.)

Goals for evaluation: Look for ability to concentrate, challenge to the body, variety and freedom of movement.

LESSONS BASED ON IMAGERY

Lessons based on the use of imagery and other stimuli could fill volumes. Here I list the types of stimuli most widely used for dance. As in the lessons on the elements, each lesson is conceived with the aid of a helper. Notice that the children's background knowledge of the elements is called upon constantly in every lesson.

In this section, the children see dance in relation to other things. This relationship will later provide them with source material for their own dances. For instance, when they see the relationship of sadness to movement, they will be able to dance their own sadness. When they see the relationship of sights and sounds to movement, they will be able to use these in expressing that feeling of sadness. If they can dance as Rumpelstiltskin would dance, then their imaginations are feeding their minds and their bodies; they will be able to dance all kinds of beings.

The use of gestures, pictures, poems, and textures should help them relate the dance in their bodies to things in the outside world. When this connection is made and strengthened, the world of dance expression is wide open before them.

Dance education is never complete. You can never say you are finished. Next year, even with the same children, if you repeat the work with the same elements and images, you will be surprised at how new it is to both you and the class. You will have changed, and your children will have grown. The lessons you develop will change and grow too. You will find a way to work that is your own and that fits the needs and abilities of your children.

The elements will always be there. The helpers you use to reach them can always be different.

LESSONS BASED ON IMAGERY

Fear

subject: feelings

helper: movement words

I'm going to say a feeling word, and I want you to show me a shape that expresses that word. The word is fear. What might make you afraid? *(Answers have been: getting caught in an elevator, getting lost, being alone in a haunted house.)* First, show me a low level shape. Go. A middle level shape. Go. High level. Go.

Now I'm going to give you movement words. Show me fear with whatever word I say. With a twist. With a turn. With a run. With a collapse. With a gallop. With a stretch. With a bend. With sharp moves. With slow moves. Fast. And hold a shape. Good.

Now instead of my movement words, use your own. Move through the space with your movement words. Do as many moves as you can that show fear. Watch out for ghosts! Go.

When you are afraid, you really use your focus—your eyes—don't you? This time we'll use music. When it begins, start in your low shape, then move through your middle and high shapes, and then move across the room. Hold your focus and your concentration. Remember, everything in your body must say "I am afraid!" When the music stops, hold your shape. Ready, go. *(Play music but only for a very short time.)* This is a very short dance, but within that short time you must show me all those moves. Don't waste time doing the same move over and over. Show me variety. How many different shapes and moves can your body do for fear? Let's try it again. Remember, eyes on your own hands, or the space around you or the walls or ceiling or floor. Don't focus on another dancer and lose your concentration. Ready, go.

Next word: silliness! Show me the silliest shape you can. Make me

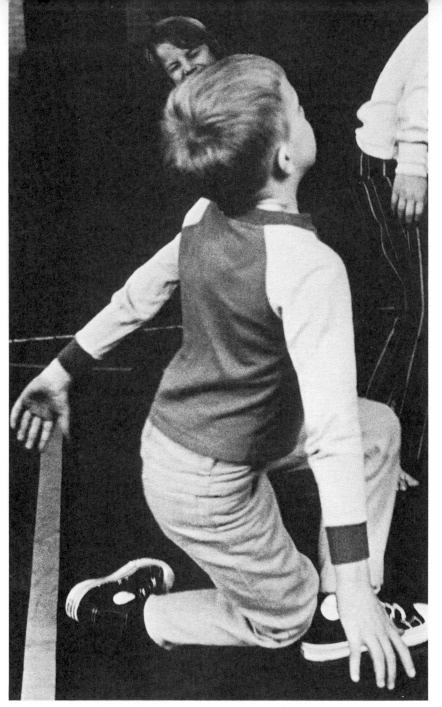

Surprise

Happiness

The beginning of the
rain dance. The children
are establishing two
focal points: "The god
of rain is up there,
and the dry ground is
down here."

see right away how silly you can be. Now a silly skip. A silly twist. A silly backward walk. A silly lift. A silly collapse. Now, on your own with the music. I'll play it only a very short time, so be prepared. Get all your silly moves in. Ready, go.

Next word: sadness. What might make you sad? Ready, shape, begin. Now that was very boring. It is dull to watch you walk around with your head down. How else can you walk besides forward? Can you walk and change levels? Can you walk on your knees? Can your focus change? As dancers you must learn how to exaggerate. What does that mean? Yes, make it bigger. Does sadness have to be slow? Does the focus always have to be down? Let's try that again and see how many changes, how much variety, you can find. Ready, go.

For the next feeling, I don't know quite what word to tell you. Let's imagine that you are in Africa. It hasn't rained for nine months. The crops are dying; the ground is bone dry. The whole village begins its rain dance ritual. This is a dance of deep concentration and belief. You must change the weather, and that takes strength of mind and body. Let me see if you can concentrate that hard. The god of rain is up there, and the dry ground is down here. Make that rain come! Remember, don't look at me or anyone else. Just keep telling that weather god the rain must come! Ready, begin. *(Use music with drums if possible.)*

For our good-bye dance today, let's do this dance of deep desire and earnest prayer. We're not in Africa anymore. We are right here. Those of you who want it to be raining when you get outside, line up over here. Those who want sun, line up over here. *(Or find two other desires.)* I'll watch to see which group is dancing with the strongest desire. And maybe when we go outside we'll see a change in the weather! Ready, go.

(Music is an additional helper in this lesson, so it is best to choose feelings for which you have appropriate music; you don't have to use these same feelings.)

Goals for evaluation: Watch whether the children dance with conviction.

What can you say with a jump? Two boys are saying "hi" while
the one on the left is saying "I've got a pain."

element: gestures

helper: please, no

Say to me with your body, "Hi!" Instead of saying hi with just one hand, say it with both. Now do it and change your level. Now turn as you make the gesture. Now turn and change your level. Make the gesture and add a step so that you move through space. Now make it huge, exaggerate it. Change your direction as you do it. Say it to all four walls.

Now say to me, with your body, "Oh, oh, oh, oooooh, I have an awful pain!" Make sure I see where that pain is. Go. Now make that gesture and change your level. Go. Turn it. Move it through space. Show me pain with a stretch. Bend. Twist. Sway. Swing. Jump. Hop. Make it bigger. Make it slower. Faster. Do it with the other side of your body. Make it small. I will play ten beats on the drum. While I'm playing those beats, dance that pain in as many ways as you can. Go. One *(count through)*, ten. *(Try "I like you," "I don't care," "I hate you," "I smell something," "Go away." See how many other gestures you and your children can think of.)*

Say to me with your body, not your voice, "please." Say it another way. How many ways can you say it with your voice? Try some of those with your body. Please. Please. Please.

Now say, "No, absolutely not!" *(Repeat several times.)* Get partners. One of you is the son or daughter, and one of you is the mother or father. The child says please as many ways as possible to get what he or she wants. The parent keeps saying no. How many ways can you say no? Do as many moves as you can think of. Move through space. Follow your parent around the house if you have to. And let me know at the end, by your movement, who wins! Practice a minute or two, and then we'll watch these duets based on gesture.

Goals for evaluation: In the duets, watch whether the children can relate to another dancer with honesty.

Three girls saying, "Oh, I have an awful pain,"
with a change of level.

subject: textures and properties

helper: bag of things

(Bring to class a bag of articles of differing textures and properties, such as a rock, a wad of cotton, a small package tied with string, some loose string, a piece of very wide elastic, a balloon. Have the children describe them in words first.) Show me the shape of this rock with your body. Now show me, if you can, its texture—how it feels to touch. It's cold, hard, smooth in part, and rough in part. Now show me in movement its heaviness, its solidness, its jagged edges.

Show me this piece of cotton with your shape. It is soft and bumpy. Can you dance like that? I can throw it and drop it without making a sound. It is curved. It can be squeezed and pulled apart easily. It is light, hardly weighs a thing. The wind could toss it easily.

Now show me the string pulled tight that binds this package. It is all straight, tight lines. All angles. No curves. Show me in space the lines that this string makes on this package.

Now show me the loose string. It flops in curved lines. It twists and curves in a light but linear way, making shapes like snakes or spaghetti.

Now show me rock, string, cotton, rock *(etc.).*

The elastic is rough and bumpy but soft. It's long and narrow. It stretches to straight and snaps back to curves. I can give this elastic a long full stretch, and let it come back slowly in a controlled way. Or I can let it snap back fast! Or I can pull it out only a small way. Show me how many ways your body can move like this elastic.

The balloon is smooth and shiny and flat. It can grow and become curved as it stretches. It can float. When I let the air out suddenly, what

"Show me the jagged edges of this big, hard, heavy rock." The girl in the center is using a low level to show the aspect of heaviness. The boy in front has used a twist of his arm to communicate the tight hardness of the rock. The girl in the back has found angular shapes with her arms alone, and the dancer on the left is expressing the bigness of the rock and using her fingers to show its tense angularity.

does it do? It dashes and dives in crazy directions to the ground. Be that balloon with your body. Go.

Now pick your favorite article. First dance its texture, what it feels like to the touch. Then dance what it looks like. And then dance what it does. Practice.

Who would like to show us and have us guess what his article is? *(Watch all who want to show.)*

Goals for evaluation: Look for the ability to capture the feeling of texture and still dance with conviction and variety.

These children are dancing to design 1. Although all of them are doing slow,
smooth, free-flowing movements, each has found a completely different way.
Besides differences in their use of space, parts of the body, and amount of
force, there is a decided difference in amount of time used. In spite of these
differences, the quality of movement is amazingly alike. Although each dancer
is dancing alone, together they form a kind of collage communicating
the same general feeling as the original design.

subject: sights

helper: designs

(Make designs out of colored construction paper. Use your own ideas.) I am going to show you a design. I don't want you to say anything out loud. I'll ask you some questions, and you answer to yourself. Here is the first design. *(Show design 1.)* Is the level low or high? Are the lines sharp or

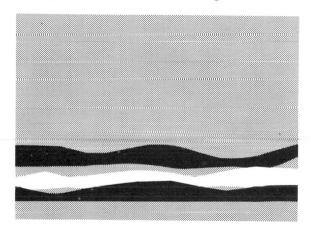

smooth? In what direction do the lines go? Now spread out on the floor and do this design in movement. Ready, starting shape, begin. Hold your shape when you think you are finished. I'll wait for everyone.

Now describe this design aloud: low level, smooth lines, continuous, flowing from side to side. Those are movement words, too, aren't they? Everyone do it again with your bodies. When you have painted this design in space with your movement, hold your shape. Ready, go.

Let's watch half the class. Notice how many different ways people can do this design. No two shapes are alike. Go. Now the other half. Go.

Notice how some people do the design quickly; others see it as slow. We all see things differently.

Now look at this design. *(Show design 2.)* Is it possible to do this in

movement? How will you do this? Think of color, force, shape, lines, direction, use of space. How do these colors make you feel? Ready, go.

Sometimes a design can produce a feeling state. Look at this one. *(Show design 3.)* I want you to dance it and get every little blob and dot

The girl at the right is holding design 4, which the group
is reflecting in movement. The boy at the bottom is making fast
small moves with his arms and hands, the center boy is moving
smoothly and slowly, and the three standing dancers are making
big swinging and swaying moves with their arms. Because
of the bright colors of the design, the children make their
moves with a lifted, upward direction.

into your movement. The way you do your blobs will show me how this design makes you feel. Ready, go.

Now each one sit near his or her favorite design, and we'll watch each design group. First, design 1. Let's see how many different ways people thought of doing this. End whenever you feel you have brought this design to life. Next design 2. Now design 3.

Let's get into groups of three or four or five people. This next design I want you to do as a group. This is design 4. *(Show the design—see the photograph on page 185.)* This time instead of each of you individually doing the design your own way, you must do it as a whole group. Take a few minutes to figure out first your starting shapes, then your movements, and then your ending shapes. Practice, and then we'll watch. *(Continue with real paintings, sculptures, scenes, the room—any sight can be transferred to dance.)*

Goals for evaluation: Watch to see whether the children are involved in their own movement. They should be moving with conviction, and should not change their moves to look like someone else.

subject: images

helper: word cards

Get into groups of three to five people. One person from each group will come and draw a card out of the bag. On the card will be a word or phrase. Your group as a whole must dance that word. For instance, your card might say "falling star." Everyone stand up and show me with just one hand how you would do falling star.

Everyone did it differently! Some had the star sparkle by moving their fingers lightly, some made the star fall in a curve, some stars fell in a straight path, some fell slowly, others fell fast. The direction was down, the force light, and it happened once and ended.

Now do "waterfall." Do it with one hand, two hands, or your whole body. Go. Okay. How is "waterfall" different from "falling star"? They both go down, don't they? Yes, but a waterfall is continuous, it is noisy, it is big and heavy, it splashes.

When you get your word, you must decide on all its characteristics. Talk about it first. Decide the size, direction, level, force, speed, where it starts, and where it ends. Then do movement that fits what you decide. As I come around, someone from each group is to draw a card. Then I'll collect the cards. Don't let other groups know your word. Take about five minutes to make up the movement. It must be exactly like your word in every respect. Then we'll watch each group, and see how close we can come to describing your word.

(Suggested words: drip, garbage disposal, umbrella, popcorn, fire, tornado, explosion, firecracker, snow, machine, melting ice cream, smoke, quicksand, a banana being eaten. It is important in this lesson to let the dancers prepare long

A first attempt at "melting ice cream." Although the children have captured the slow, smooth, downward quality, they have not found the unevenness in design or time, or the collapsed quality. In order to form a beginning shape, they joined hands. This caused some tension and some evenness in movement to remain, and made it more difficult for them to move isolated parts of their bodies. Comments from the observers helped reveal to the dancers the many qualities inherent in melting ice cream.

enough so that they relate every aspect of the word to movement. Go around and help the groups by asking them questions relating to the elements.

Teach the audience not to guess merely at random what the word is. They should rather follow your example by saying things such as, "I saw light, airy movement with the direction upward and outward. It started all together, then separated, and finally disappeared. It went from medium to slow and it had a breath quality." That would be a good movement description of smoke. If the audience comes up with that description, then the dancers have been highly successful! If a group is unsuccessful, have the audience decide what characteristic is missing or poorly done. The audience can then direct the changes, and the performing group should repeat the study. This is excellent training for perception of movement and the relationship of movement to other things. The audience training is as important as the training of the dancers.

You can continue with images that arise from the children's studies, trips, or ideas.)

Goals for evaluation: Look for ability to work with a group and to relate the elements of movement to a word.

"Rise as you make your sound. If it's a smooth sound, rise smoothly.
If it's a staccato sound, rise with sharp, short jerks."

subject: sounds

helper: voices

Think of the sound of the clock. Now make that sound. *(Make a clicking sound.)* That is a rather small, light sound, but sharp. Now make a small, light, sharp move every time you make that ticking sound. Go.

Make the sound of the alarm on the clock. Who can describe that sound? Long, continuous, piercing, loud, vibrant, high. Okay. Do a long, unending, vibrating, high level move. Go.

Make the sound of a motor starting, any kind of motor. Repeat it in movement. From short, sharp spurts to smooth flowing.

What other sounds can you make and do in movement too? *(Answers have been: sirens, water boiling, a kettle hissing, coughing, moaning, sneezing, sighing, screaming, laughing, birds, wind.)*

Everyone take a low level. This time you can make any sound you want to—any at all. It doesn't have to be *like* anything. It can be a sound you never made before or you never heard before. As you make the sound, rise to high level. If your sound is smooth, rise smoothly. If it's jerky, jerk to high level. Make as many sounds as you need to get to high level. Go.

Now make a new sound, a completely different sound, and return to low level. Try it again. Make at least two sounds: one to get you up and one to get you back down. This time make the moves interesting. Add a turn, a hop, or some interesting shapes. The sound and the movements must be exactly together and exactly the same. Body sounds and body movements. Ready, all together, go.

This is crazy, isn't it? Don't worry if it is crazy. Just think how you'll be able to accompany your own dances! Make louder sounds this time, and then change to softer ones. See if you can react with your movements. Go. Let's watch and listen to these. We'll go right around the room. Make your sound, and do your movement. Don't mind if we laugh!

Now we're going to make sound machines! Divide into groups of three, four, or five. Make a group dance using at least four sounds. Make the four sounds as different as possible, so that the movements will be as different as possible. Decide how many times you'll do each sound, and how long each sound will last. Everyone in the group can do the sounds simultaneously, or perhaps you'll want just one to do a sound. Use variety in planning it. Remember: all of you in the group are one sound machine. Make your shapes and movements fit together like pieces of one machine. Get your starting shape, sounds and movements, and ending shape. Work for about five minutes, and then we'll watch these unique sound machines! *(Sound machines can be done with real or handmade instruments or recorded sound effects as well as live sound effects.)*

Goals for evaluation: Look for free use of voice as well as movement.

subject: qualities

helper: what's in the cage

Who has seen a lion? Show me how a lion moves. Now show me how a cat moves. What is the difference between a lion and a cat? Now can you stand on two feet and move like a lion? Can you still get that movement in your back? Can you still move your head and make your eyes piercing and creep stealthily with your paws? Show me how a lion leaps or runs. Show me how it sleeps. Show me another resting lion shape. How does a lion use its paws? Are they big or little? What happens to a cat's back when it is angry or frightened? Show me.

Now show me a snake. Show me that wiggling snake but, instead of moving along the ground, keep the feeling of a snake and move upward to high level. Can you do that? It must still be smooth and curved and darting—like a snake, but like a dancer too. We are dancers, so we must be able to get the quality of snake into our bodies. We don't pretend we are snakes, we dance the quality of snake.

Now everyone line up on the black line, and go across the floor two or three at a time. You must walk, but you can move as a snake or as a lion. Let me see what you are.

Everyone spread out in the room and build a cage around yourself. You are now in a zoo. What are you? Don't be a lion or a snake, we've done those. Be something else. What will you be? A bear? A flamingo? A lizard? Does everyone have an idea? Good. First show me how your animal rests. Go. Show me another resting shape. Go. Now show me that animal moving at low level. Can it turn? Now change levels and keep the feeling or the quality or the essence of that animal in your body.

"Build a cage around yourself. You are now in a zoo. What are you?"
Here a child uses alternating bent and twisted but smooth arm movements,
gradually coming forward to give the quality of an alligator's walk.

Go. Now move around inside your cage. How does your animal feel being caged? Imagine your cage being opened. Does your animal rush out? Or does it slowly come out? How does it move? What would it do if it met a person? Would it want to be petted? Run away? Eat him up? Imagine a person in front of you. What do you do?

This time I am not going to tell you what to do or suggest things you can do. You must do all the things that will help us to get the feeling or quality of your animal. I will come around and open your cage. You can move in your cage and out of your cage. Be sure to change levels. When you return to your cage, we'll guess what you are!

(It is important that the children understand how to use the movements of the animals as dancers. A dancer uses all the elements while portraying the animal, thus giving the feeling or the essence of the animal rather than pretending to "be" the animal. The goal is to communicate a quality. Continue with other things in nature that have a distinctive quality. African music makes this lesson exciting!)

Goals for evaluation: Look for the ability to select and convey an animal quality.

Each child is dancing Rumpelstiltskin moving around his imaginary fire. "This time add a turn or a jump as you dance around the fire." The children gradually increase their vocabulary of steps and moves, from plain skipping to adding body shapes and changes of level. Then they select those they will keep as part of their Rumpelstiltskin dance.

subject: stories and poems

helper: Rumpelstiltskin

(The important thing about using stories and poems is to make them short enough. Take only part of a well-known story, so that interest is focused on development of movement rather than on sequential happenings. Two or three visual images or feelings are plenty to work with. In this lesson, begin by discussing the story of Rumpelstiltskin up to the part where he is dancing around his fire singing about his name.) First, show me your fire. Walk around it so I can see how big it is. Spread out so no one walks into anyone else's fire.

Rumpelstiltskin is a funny, little man. Show me how he would skip around his fire. Take eight counts. Go. Do you suppose he would skip so evenly with no body shape? What kind of body shape would he have? Can you hop around your fire this time in that body shape? Go. Next, try a turn or a jump with those hops. Go. Can he change his body shape as he dances? Remember: he is a strange, little gnome. Maybe his shoulders move. How would he move his hands? Where would his face be looking as he dances? Go.

This time dance in one spot, behind your fire, using your face, your hands, your shoulders, your hips, and changing levels, but staying on one spot. Go. One *(count through),* eight. Now let's do eight counts around the fire and eight counts behind the fire. I'll sing for you this time:

> Rumpelstiltskin, Rumpelstiltskin, Rumpelstiltskin, is
>   my name.
> Rumpelstiltskin, Rumpelstiltskin, Rumpelstiltskin,
>   ha, ha, ha!

(I have simplified the song that Rumpelstiltskin sings in the story. The authentic verse is:

> *Merrily the feast I'll make*
> *Today I'll brew, tomorrow I'll bake*
> *Merrily I'll dance and sing*
> *For next day will a stranger bring*
> *Little does my lady dream*
> *Rumpelstiltskin is my name.)*

Let me see these dances: first this half of the class. *(Performance and comments.)* Next half. *(Performance and comments.)*

Next comes the queen's emissary, who asks, "Is your name Bandylegs?"

Rumpelstiltskin laughs and says, "No." How can you laugh with your body? How can you say, "No"?

"Is your name Crookshanks?"

"No."

"Is your name Rumpelstiltskin?" And what does Rumpelstiltskin do then? He stamps and stamps and stamps himself right through the ground and disappears forever! How would you do that?

(I often make up strange and different names besides Bandylegs and Crookshanks, as this surprises and pleases the children. Always feel free to make changes that will better suit your needs.)

Now let's do the whole story. The queen sent her emissary to find out the little fellow's name. While wandering through the countryside, he hears:

> Rumpelstiltskin, Rumpelstiltskin, Rumpelstiltskin is
>   my name,
> Rumpelstiltskin, Rumpelstiltskin, Rumpelstiltskin,
>   ha, ha, ha!

"Aha, there! Is your name Bandylegs?"

"No."

"Is your name Crookshanks?"

"No."

"Is your name Rumpelstiltskin?"

"Ooooooooh, ooooooooh, ooooooooh!" And he was never seen again!

Shall we watch each half of the class? *(Performance and comments.)*

Now let's divide into groups. *(Continue with four or five selections from one of these categories: nursery rhymes, haiku poetry, other literature, or original stories or poems. Have each group choose a selection. On another day, use another category.)* Find shapes and movements that fit the images produced by the words. Work five minutes, and then we'll watch.

Goals for evaluation: Look for dancing with joy and involvement as well as with variety.

5

Extending the Lessons

RESPONDING TO THE INDIVIDUAL STUDENT

Children show us in many ways that they want to relate to us individually, not as part of the group. Respond to this need. As often as you can, challenge an individual child. We are all eager to be treated as single persons, not just members of a class.

Besides learning and using each child's name sometime during each class, try to find one area in which you can compliment each child. You might say, "Rachel, with her good ear for sound," or "Joe, our jumper," or "Babette, with the smiling face." It doesn't have to be a dance comment; it is a personal comment. The children feel special because you have seen them as individuals.

Throw out a challenge or a question, something the children can do, if they wish, on their own time before the next class. If a child does respond, use that response in class or work further with that student.

Give likely children special projects; entice less responsive children by relating dance to something that interests them. You might try asking the children to write down their names and something in which they are interested. Perhaps they know sports or like horses. Take the slips home, note the ideas (especially from the hard-to-reach children), and start with these. Make a lesson plan finding the relationship of movement to the interest of a child. Ask brilliant children to give *you* help, to describe movements of protons and electrons, to describe the workings of an automobile engine, to compose accompaniment for a dance.

Here is a sample list of interests from fifth graders: reading, soccer, baseball, military history, Russia, birds, horses, camping, knitting, stamps. Very briefly, you might connect them to dance in the following ways:

Reading: a. Ask the children to call out action words (verbs) from a favorite book, such as striking, turning, growing, falling. Do the same with descriptive words (adverbs) such as roughly, proudly, crazily, merrily. Write the words on small cards. Have the children draw one from each pile and dance the combination (such as striking proudly, growing crazily, turning merrily, or falling roughly).

   b. Collect rhyming words such as bright, kite, height, might, fight, light. Make a contest, a game, or a show out of moving as the words.

   c. Gather all the words describing the action of a selected noun. For example, take "fire": fire shoots out, rages, subsides, crackles, grows, smolders, destroys. Then choose adverbs or "how" words—furiously, uncontrollably, swiftly, suddenly, gradually, slowly. Make a three-part dance with chosen combinations: (1) the fire smolders slowly, (2) it suddenly rages, (3) it gradually subsides.

   d. Make a dance from a small part of a favorite story.

Soccer, baseball: Take the actions used in these sports. Try them in slow motion; try them backwards. Repeat them, combine them rhythmically. Change the use of force or energy. In this way, put the sport into dance form. Discuss differences between dance and sports.

Military history: Use formations such as left flank, right flank, and center. Arrange offense and defense (groups facing each other) and have them do question and answer movements stressing change of level, use of force, and focus. Perhaps the student can choreograph a famous battle.

Russia: Have the children describe the Russian terrain by changes in level. Different sections of the room can be different regions. Perhaps one part of Russian history can be danced.

Birds: Discuss what happens to migrating birds. "Do they all make it? Do birds follow a leader? A pathway? How do birds walk? How do they move their heads? What is involved in learning to fly? Do you have a Jonathan Livingston Seagull in your class?"

Horses: Discuss what steps horses can do. "What steps can the dancing Lippizan horses do? How do stable horses move? How do wild horses move?"

Camping: Vary the movements of hiking, woodchopping, canoeing, and tenting by slow motion or by changing the rhythm, the space, or the force. Shapes of constellations can be made, accompanied by night sounds.

Knitting: Arrange the class in partners or small groups. How many ways can they find to move "in," "over," "through," and "off," the cue words for learning to knit.

Stamps: Perhaps the student can tell you about his or her most valuable stamp. Begin by having groups make the shape of the stamp and the design. The subject can then come alive, dance its character, and return to the stamp.

This method of relating subjects to dance is just one way to try to interest the individual child in your class. The more deeply you go into one subject, the more meaningful it is to all the children. A once-over-lightly treatment is not satisfying. It is better to do one or two subjects in depth than to attempt to do several superficially. The superficial treatment may reach only the child whose hobby it is. The deep treatment can reach all the children, because they will have spent time and effort and will in the end have contributed their ideas too.

RELATING DANCE TO OTHER AREAS IN LIFE

Modern American society is one of the few in which there is no dance essential to the culture. Many countries still dance wedding rituals that have been handed down from ancestors. Agricultural and work dances, religious and magical dances are still done in many parts of the world, if not for their original function still as an important part of the life of the people. In the United States, most of our dance is social or theatrical. Perhaps the closest we come to depth of expression through movement by ordinary people is creative educational dance. Let the children feel this importance by relating their dance to events that mean something in their daily lives, or that touch chords of emotional feeling.

I watched a skilled teacher do a class that involved lots of skips, leaps, gallops, and combinations of these. The children's bodies were involved in total physical movement, and their minds were busy counting and placing the moves.

Then he asked them to sit down cross-legged with straight backs. The attention of the children was captured by this abrupt change of pace. The teacher then proceeded to lead them in very simple, stylized, unison movements of the hands, arms, and head. He accompanied them with his voice and with a soft, even, almost hypnotic drumbeat. The quiet formality seemed to lend dignity and meaning to the movement. The children felt it. A hush seemed to envelop them. They were no longer moving only physically and mentally. They were involved emotionally.

This is difficult to do, but very important. We need to bring each class to a point where the children can feel what it means to dance, to use themselves fully in mind, body, and spirit. To do this, we must somehow reach their emotions. Sometimes this happens through the drama of an idea. Sometimes the poetry they write for their dance evokes inner feeling. Sometimes the music you play makes a difference. Let them not think dance is merely a challenge to physical skill.

Human beings are not fragmented pieces; the emotions are tied to movement. When we move, we feel, and when we feel, we are moved. Aim for feeling states through movement.

holidays

For some, dance becomes more meaningful when it relates to another subject. Try using holidays in your dance class. It's hard to get past October 31 without a Halloween dance! Some lessons that fit this theme easily are lesson 5, living sculpture (you can change the name to rising ghosts); lesson 8, graveyard; lesson 17, spaghetti monsters, and lesson 19, haunted house. Children love to do a good-bye dance acting out the movements of the character they plan to be on Halloween.

If you like to use the children's ideas, you might start by asking them what kinds of characters are out on Halloween night. Take one at a time. How do they move? (See the section on structuring an idea, page 39.) After finding all possible movement qualities in several ideas, combine two by saying, "Once upon a time, late at night, there were some black cats moving about. Suddenly some ghosts appeared. Then what happened? How shall we end this dance?"

When Thanksgiving draws near, and you feel the need for a Thanksgiving dance, why not use the coming of the *Mayflower*? Discuss how it must have tossed as it sailed the rough ocean. Imagine the fear and curiosity of the Pilgrims, and the silent, alert, watchful movements of the Indians. Think about the ritual of the feast. What is a ritual?

In order to make a dance and not a play, ask for movement words that describe the action. Ask for one movement word to describe the ocean and the ship — it might be rolling. One movement word to describe the Indians—it might be darting. One movement word to describe the ritual of friendship and thanks—it might be joining hands. Then, remembering crossovers (page 34), make a three-part dance: (1) rolling (stressing perhaps changes of level, and using high rolling with jumps as well as middle level and floor rolls), (2) darting (using sharp movements and straight short pathways), and (3) joining hands (their own hands, each other's hands, contact shapes in small groups and finally in one large group for an ending).

Christmas is a time of beautiful music and happy feelings. Traditional carols have very clear rhythmic patterns that can be translated into moves and steps. If you are working with older children, give small groups each a phrase of a familiar tune. Have them set steps to its rhythm. Use entrances and exits. The resulting dance with each group performing successively can be exciting!

With smaller children, instead of what's in the cage, for lesson 33, you might try what's in the package? First, have the children explore many ideas by working on mechanical toy movements, rag doll moves, or computer workings. Then let them each dance the toy of their choice.

Valentine's Day is ever popular with children. Have them discuss what happens to their hearts when they get excited. It goes faster, of course. (See lesson 16, fast and slow.) Relate this to movement: "Can you show me a movement that gets faster? Now find a very slow beat, and then make that move go faster. Make the shape of a heart with your whole body. Can you make a heart shape with a partner? Can you rock that shape? Can you make those moves change speed? Can you move your heart shape through space? Change levels? Can the whole class make one huge heart shape in the room? Can you show the lace around the edges?"

For Easter explore the accents in "Happy Easter" (see lesson 22, accent). In that rhythm, have the rabbits jump, the spring showers fall, and the flowers grow. Have the children spell out Easter by making the letters with their bodies. They can paint the word in the air and write it on the floor with a pathway.

academic subjects

When relating academic subjects to dance, think of relating to one element in particular. Use the element to help teach the subject, or the subject to help teach the element. Use crossovers (page 34) to make the lesson thorough, and be sure to put the learning into some kind of form with a finish. In other words, structure such a lesson as you would if you were starting from the element itself.

It is possible to teach verbs, adverbs, rhyming words; addition, subtraction, fractions, parts and whole; cursive writing and printing; geometric shapes; forms of matter, laws of motion, nuclear action, chemical action, mechanical laws; history, geography, geology; and more. Find which elements to use by asking the class:

How does this subject relate to space: shape, level, direction, size, pathway, place?

How does this subject relate to time: beat, speed, duration, pattern?

How does this subject relate to force: attack, strength, weight, flow?

Can you imitate or feel such actions in your body?

Can the class imitate such actions as a group?

After the exploration, complete the lesson by putting the actions into a form (see page 36).

current events

Someday, in spite of your careful planning, you may have to or want to build a lesson spontaneously. Something will happen that interests the children so much you'll want to make it part of the lesson for the day. For instance, if a sudden thunderstorm comes up, if the electricity goes off, if a favorite friend is leaving the school, if a dance company has performed at the school, or if the children have just seen a popular movie, you'll want to use these things. Structure spontaneous happenings just as you would structure ideas from the children (see page 39). When something looms large in the lives of the children, by all means, build a lesson around it. Don't hesitate. Find your way by trial and error. You'll do better tomorrow by starting today!

USING PLAY

Laughter and play are the fertile soil of learning. When a spirit of laughter and play pervades a dance class, learning is encouraged. Use dance games on rainy days, on days when your lesson takes a shorter time than you expected, and for classes whose attention span wanes.

You will find times when a game seems to emerge either at the start, during, or at the end of a class. Play is a needed balance to work, and it is also an effective tool in learning. Use it when you can.

Think of the following games not as set activities that you must follow, but rather as ideas that grew with happenings in a class. They can change and be changed.

stick together

One day a couple of six year olds came to class arm in arm announcing, "We're stuck together," and they laughed. I combined their predicament with an old game, and it took hold. Now other classes enjoy it. Here is how it goes.

Play a record. All dance. You can have the children free dance (page 44) or work on the element for the day. When the music stops, call out, "Toe to toe," and all must touch their toes to someone else's toes. Start the music again and again they all dance. Stop the music and call out, "Knee to knee," or "Back to back," or "Elbow to elbow." They can match one other person, or a group of others. Finally call out, "Stick together!" and they must find different ways in twos or in groups to make group shapes, touching any way they want to. Sometimes a whole class sticks together. They find this delightful.

see me

I learned this from a colleague (Roberta Bristol, Cabrillo College, Aptos, California), who noticed the need small children have to be watched. How often do you hear, "Like this?" and "Watch me!" Here is how the game goes.

All the children hide their eyes. One child is chosen to be It and tiptoes someplace in the room. It calls out, "See me." All open their eyes and find It. It then says, "Be like me." and all mirror Its shape. "Move like me." All follow Its movement. "Come to me." All run to Its place, where a new child is chosen to be It, and the game begins again.

corners

This game has many variations. Here are two.

Number the corners. All dance. When the music stops, all run to a corner, any corner. One child then draws a number from a hat, and all in that corner are eliminated. The game continues until only a few or one child remains. The element of luck, the simplicity, and the quickness of this game delight the children.

When the number of children still dancing is reduced to two, eliminate two corners and announce that the two dancers must choose different corners. The last child remaining, the "winner," can lead the line, be first to play your drum, or choose the next activity.

"Corners" can also be used as an ending to class. Those in the corner called can be the first to go put their shoes on. In this way, all the children become "winners" as their corner is called, and no one is "eliminated."

In the second variation, corners need not be numbered. This is a contest between you and the children. The group is in the center of the room. You give them a challenge, and they see if they can do it while you turn your back and count to five. Challenges can be:

Be evenly divided in all four corners.

Be equally divided, but in two corners.

Make a diagonal line between two corners.

Five in each corner, the rest in the center.

Everyone wearing blue in one corner, tan in another, red in another, green in another. The rest in the center.

Depending upon the age and the wardrobe of your class, you'll think of many more challenges.

pictures

This game is best with older children, as they must be able to work as a group and to see themselves as a single entity.

Divide the class into two or three groups. You can give them all the same picture to make, or you can give them each a different one. Pictures can be of Washington crossing the Delaware, King Tut in his tomb, the Spirit of St. Louis, the Statue of Liberty, a Christmas tree, a car, a pyramid, the Golden Gate Bridge, a tunnel, an accident scene, etc. Each group works on making the picture, using all the bodies in the group. When the group is ready, the members sit or lie down or move apart. On cue, they snap into position and hold. This is the fun of it—suddenly they become a single picture instead of a number of people.

can you?

The competition in dance is between an individual child and what she or he is capable of being. But sometimes it's fun to use the elements of dance to compete against another team as in a race.

Divide the class into four or five teams. Number the members of the teams. Then give all the number ones a challenge combining a step plus a movement of a body part. When they have raced, the winner can be given a point, and you then continue with the next in line.

Challenges can be:

Can you turn your head from side to side while you hop? Go.

Can you arch and round your back while walking on your toes? Go.

Can you stretch and bend your arms while you gallop? Go.

Can you circle your arms outwardly and slide sideward? Go.

Can you rotate your arms and jump? Go.

Can you squat and walk with your arms stretched upward and circle your hands?

Can you run backward, look backward, and point forward?

Can you shake your whole body and skip?

You can give each winner a point, or you can have the children do each set just for fun. Children enjoy helping you make up challenges.

quick commands

This can be an elimination game, but it can also be done just for fun. Give three commands, then say go. The children must wait until you say go. Then they must execute the commands as quickly as they can. Make the last command a change in level or place so that you can see who is first and who is last clearly. Suggested commands:

Spin around, run and touch a wall, come back and sit.

Touch your head to the floor, jump up, sit down.

Spin around, clap your hands, stand up.

Jump and turn, sit, skip to a wall.

Scratch your ear, roll your head, kneel.

criss-cross town

Young children enjoy this simple game. Before playing it, have them work first on twisting and crossing movements.

A few children are in the center of the room. Others hide in far corners.

"Once upon a time, some children fell asleep in a park. But they didn't know the park was in Criss-Cross Town! Suddenly, out from behind trees, out from under rocks came the curious Criss-Cross people. There were Criss-Cross dogs and Criss-Cross spiders, Criss-Cross cats and Criss-Cross rabbits, Criss-Cross men and Criss-Cross women, Criss-Cross boys and Criss-Cross girls.

"Sometimes they crawled sideward, sometimes backward, sometimes turning, but always with crossing movements. They came closer and closer to the sleeping children, when—suddenly—the children awoke and stretched. They stretched so high and so wide, it frightened the Criss-Cross people and they criss-crossed back to their hiding places just as fast as they could!"

The first ones back can be the new stretching children, or you can simply choose the next.

Feel free to make up games as you go along. Sometimes spur-of-the-moment games that last only a few minutes can be of value to the class. Use your game-making skills as they suit your purpose!

DEMONSTRATING THE PROCESS AND THE PRODUCT

In creative dance we like to think that the process is more important than the product, that the experience of creating movement is an end in itself. I believe this is true. There are times when children rehearse something they have created, and the life seems to go out of it. They no longer seem involved the way they originally did. They seem to be imitating their former selves. Adults, on the other hand, improve with rehearsal.

Yet we do want to perform to let parents, teachers, and other students see what is happening. We want to share our successes and show the progress of the children. What is the answer?

I find that the best demonstrations are often actual classes rather than performances. The children might have had a previous lesson like the one they are doing for an audience, but the teacher is finding new words, new challenges, so the students' actions are spontaneous. A skilled teacher can do this in front of an audience and keep the children secure at the same time. Such a demonstration class is perhaps the best way to share children's dance accomplishments.

However, if you feel you would like a prepared performance by the children, where you say nothing except perhaps the title and a brief description, here are some simple ways to proceed. These simple forms can be accompanied by your drum or by recorded music.

extension of the good-bye dance

Line the children up at the far end of the stage or auditorium. Have them dance one at a time, making pathways that fill the space. Each should end at a certain spot and make a shape. When one has finished, the next dancer begins. The last dancer moves in and out zigzagging through the still shapes, and then leads the class single-file in a full circle to the exit.

This simple one-at-a-time form has endless variations. Masking tape on the floor or an "obstacle course" of small props can help the children remember to dance in diverse pathways. "Magic spots" can be designated, and at these special places they know to do kicks, jumps, turns, and their most exciting movement inventions.

Such a dance can be entitled "Summer Fun" and can be billed as a happy dance with children looking forward to summer vacation. Or one child can be dressed as king or queen and the others can all be dancing for royalty. Children usually perform well when allowed to dance freely on their own, with some clear idea in mind.

movement in succession

This is the next simplest form of performance. Number the children individually or number groups of children. All begin on stage in shapes. Number one dances and ends off to the side. Each succeeding child or group of children continues in turn. When all have finished and are at the sides of the stage space, they come to the center and make a group shape. This ending can be done with a flourish!

We once used this form for a dance called, "This program is brought to you by the letter S." The children were seated in the form of a big letter S. They had worked on movement words beginning with S, such as stretch, skip, sway, and on nonmovement words beginning with S, such a smile, sizzle, soft. Each had chosen a favorite word and set of movements. One by one they rose and performed as their word was announced. Each dancer ended off to the side. After the last child had finished, all ran to the center and reformed the giant letter S.

solo in the circle

This third form for dance presentation also takes little preparation. The children are seated in a circle and take turns leading hand and arm shapes. Play a drum beat or musical accompaniment with three or four beats to a measure; that is, one, two, three, or one, two, three, four. The leader moves hands and arms to a shape on count one. All the other children mirror the shape simultaneously, then they hold for the rest of the measure. If it is a four beat, the count would be shape, hold, hold, hold. When the leader has done three or four hand shapes, she or he looks at the next person, and that person becomes the leader. Any child who does not want to lead simply looks at the following child, and the movement continues.

This circle choral movement accompanies a dancer in the center. Whoever has been previously chosen to be the first dancer in the center begins. He or she dances for a while, then sits and joins the group as the succeeding center dancers take their turns. This form is effective for rain dances (see page 175) and other ritual ideas.

birds and trees

All begin on stage in a shape (trees). One dancer (a bird) begins to move through space, in and out among the trees. Another begins, then another and another. (You can call names or clothing colors, or the order can be set ahead of time.) Soon all are dancing. When this happens, the first dancer stops, followed by the next and the next, until all have stopped in still shapes.

This form is good for dance ideas other than birds and trees, if they have a surging climax and a long, slow, fading end (a storm, the ocean, the wind, a catastrophe, etc.).

Notice that all the forms described so far are basically follow-the-leader forms. How many more follow-the-leader ideas can you think of? I'm sure you'll think of several.

group improvisation

If the class has had some practice in contact improvisation (touching, supporting, and making shapes with other bodies) and if the children can stop and go on their own, then group improvisation becomes a usable form for demonstration of creative movement.

All begin in a single group shape, touching, but with lots of air spaces. One child or a few children break away and move around and through the still shape. When they feel like it, others move. Whenever dancers stop, they form new shapes by contact. Older children do well at this, as they know to keep the space filled, either with moving shapes or with contact still shapes. Fade the music to indicate the children should form an ending shape.

In addition to using these simple basic forms, you can demonstrate your children's dance by using any form that results from the lessons in this book, or from lessons that you develop spontaneously or prepare from other stimuli. Remember, however, that these dance demonstrations by the children are all improvised. We are not teaching the children to compose dances. That exciting next step can come later.

6
Closing Notes

THE DRUM

A drum (and its percussive friends) can add magic to a class. Children love a drum and can learn much from its use. If you have the opportunity to do so, by all means incorporate a drum into your sessions. I have a drum and a felt-tipped drumstick. I beat both the head and the rim.

At the end of the class, I allow the child who gets shoes and socks on first to play the drum. Whoever wants to play it next lines up behind the first child, and so on. If there is enough time, most of the children have a chance to play. I never let them play the drum freely before class starts, only at the end. I keep my drum as my "greater noise" that controls other noises—until the end of class.

Besides this everyday free activity, I often use the drum as a quiet activity. We sit in a circle and I play an even beat (with young children) or I beat my name or an interesting pattern for older children. The group claps with the drum. Then I pass the drum to the next person. That child plays as he or she wishes, loud or soft, fast or slow, a beat or a pattern, and we clap just the way the drum is played.

When this system becomes established, I ask the children one at a time to decide how we should respond to the drum other than by clapping (which has no variety). Sometimes they clap on their heads or the floor. Sometimes they beat their feet together or their elbows. Sometimes they dance with their shoulders or ribs. As the drum changes hands, so does the movement leader. Sometimes, while one child is beating the drum, another dances around the outside of the circle and back to place. Such use of the drum can be inserted into the lesson at any time.

This same general pattern can be used with a variety of sounds from instruments that you bring to class. The qualities in sound are closely related to the qualities in movement, and some children will be stimulated to make and play their own instruments.

Variety in accompaniment helps. Adding even one or two sounds (played by the children, perhaps) to your constant drum can generate excitement. Many schools have sets of rhythm instruments that include maracas, drums, tambourines, claves (rhythm sticks), triangles, cymbals, woodblocks, and guiros. In addition, a variety of useful percussion instruments can be made. New and different uses of sounds for accompaniment are especially welcome in the lessons based on imagery.

Keep the instruments handy. Use them often. Experiment, feel free and at ease with them. Your drumming proficiency will grow with practice and repetition, as will your skill in teaching dance!

RECORDS

Before you buy any records or use anyone's suggestions, check the records that you already own. You probably have a variety and can use bits and pieces from selections with which you are already familiar. Also check the reverse sides of your school's folk dance records. You may find very usable, clearly rhythmic music.

The public library is often a good source of records. I suggest you look through listings of collections, anthologies, and the like, because often such records contain a series of short pieces that are easy to locate while you are in the midst of a class. Look under "dance" or "children" in the card catalog, and you might find some surprises. Listen to a local classical radio station; it can familiarize you with names of composers whose works you can then look up at the library.

There are numerous records made especially for teachers of dance and numerous records of ballet music shortened and simplified for children. Catalogs of these can be found at supply houses such as:

Children's Music Center
5373 West Pico Boulevard, Los Angeles, California 90019

Pacific Dance Supplies
1630 Taraval Street, San Francisco, California 94116

Dance Etc.
5897 College Avenue, Oakland, California 94618

Folk dance records and children's records can be found at:

Festival Folk Shop
160 Turk Street, San Francisco, California 94102

Folk Dance House
P.O. Box 201, Flushing, New York 11352

Folkraft Dance Record Center
10 Fenwick Street, Newark, New Jersey 07114

Phil Maron's Folk Shop
1531 Clay Street, Oakland, California 94612

Worldtone Music, Inc.
230 Seventh Avenue, New York, New York 10011

And don't forget to check the local listings in the yellow pages of the telephone directory, under "Records—phonograph—retail."

Remember that recorded music is only incidental to the lesson at hand. We do not prepare or set dances to the music. Music is used for follow-the-leader starts, improvisational exploration, free dancing, and the good-bye dances. Composing dances to music is a completely different thing.

Bibliography

Andrews, Gladys. *Creative Rhythmic Movement for Children.* New York: Prentice-Hall, 1954.

Barlin, Anne, and Barlin, Paul. *The Art of Learning through Movement.* Los Angeles: Ward Ritchie Press, 1971.

Boorman, Joyce. *Creative Dance in the First Three Grades.* New York: David McKay Co., 1969.

Canner, Norma. *And a Time to Dance.* Boston: Beacon Press, 1968.

Cherry, Clare. *Creative Movement for the Developing Child.* Belmont, Calif.: Fearon Publishers, 1969.

Dimondstein, Geraldine. *Children Dance in the Classroom.* New York: Macmillan Co., 1971.

Jones, Genevieve. *Seeds of Movement.* Pittsburgh: Volkwein Bros., 1973.

King, Bruce. *Creative Movement.* New York: Bruce King Studio, 1968.

Laban, Rudolf. *Modern Educational Dance.* London: Macdonald and Evans, 1963.

Monsour, Sally; Cohen, Marilyn; and Lindell, Patricia. *Rhythm in Music and Dance for Children.* Belmont, Calif.: Wadsworth Publishing Co., 1966.

Murray, Ruth Lovell. *Dance in Elementary Education.* New York: Harper and Row, 1962.

Russell, Joan. *Creative Dance in the Primary School.* New York: Frederick Praeger Publishers, 1968.

Wiener, Jack, and Lidstone, John. *Creative Movement for Children.* New York: Van Nostrand Reinhold Co., 1969.

Winters, Shirley. *Creative Rhythmic Movement.* Dubuque, Iowa: William C. Brown Co., 1975.

Acknowledgments

The source material for this book is derived from the teachings of the great movement analyst Rudolf Laban and his followers. In addition, I wish to acknowledge Ruth Beckford, Gertrude Blanchard, and Juan Valenzuela, teachers from whom I learned so much and who, with many others, will see their influence in these pages.

To Susan Burack, friend, fellow teacher, and willing mentor, I am especially grateful for giving of her knowledge, her insight, her ideas, and her discoveries, and for sharing the concern that nurtured the development of this book.

My gratitude is also extended to Jo-Anne Smithmeyer and the Indianapolis Department of Parks and Recreation for giving me the freedom and the opportunity to write; to Lenore Thompson for her encouragement and direction; and to Annette Macdonald for her interest and confidence.

Finally, my thanks go to Sister Rita Lechner and the children of Holy Cross Central School whose pictures helped me tell the story:

222

Marilyn Arimado
Valerie Beikman
Rhonda Church
Juanita Fernandez
Gregory Frazee
Theresa Gin
Amy Groth
Kevin Hamilton
Michael Jones
Terri Lynn Jones
Lisa Kennedy
Donald Nevins
Lamont Patterson
Catherine Pranger
Kathleen Russell
Frederick Serviss
Kathleen Tobin
Michael Walls
Garrick Walton
Lisa Wilson

Patty Alsip
Tonny Ardizzone
Arnold Dumaual
Jimmy Fitzgerald
Florence Gin
Lawrence Gin
Johnny Hahn
Francis Hammans
Thomas Hammans
Patty Higgins
Felice Knarr
Eddie O'Connor
Stephanee Perry
Bertha Shea
Crystal Taylor
Michelle Taylor
Stacy Thompson
Joyce Walls
Edwin Wilmowski
Donald Wooldridge

"Why
do you
dance?"

"Something
inside me tells
me that I love
it and to keep
going on and
on because I
love it so much.
I never want to
stop. I want to
tell the whole
world about
something. . . ."

Index